To David,
You are an
incredible asset
to every company lucky
enough to work with you!
My Best to you,
Warmly
Betsy

BE
BOARD
READY

BE
BOARD
READY

THE SECRETS TO LANDING A BOARD SEAT AND BEING A GREAT DIRECTOR

BETSY ATKINS

Serial Entrepreneur, three-time CEO, Digitization and
Corporate Governance Expert

I dedicate this book to future board members and entrepreneurs who have the courage to build great companies for their shareholders.

- Betsy Atkins

"Betsy Atkins is uniquely qualified to teach how to accelerate building better boards that continuously extend shareholder value creation. As Independent Lead Director at HD Supply and Nominating & Governance Committee Chair, Betsy leads the charge on creating exceptional board of directors composition and dynamics. In today's environment of activism, global volatility, and both strengthening and emerging competitive threats, rapid, world-class board execution is essential to navigating a winning path forward. Betsy's overwhelming passion to apply hard work, opportunistically identify and engage an extended network of expert talent, and direct board activity to be an incredible business asset and accelerant is a most powerful playbook."

 - **Joseph J. DeAngelo, Chairman & CEO, HOME DEPOT SUPPLY**

"Fulfilling director responsibilities during a company's best times can be challenging. Betsy Atkins had the courage to join our board as an Independent Director during a time of company crisis. Betsy provided not only a steady hand but also the focused, strategic thinking and experience in corporate governance necessary to navigate a clear path forward. Betsy's understanding of best-in-class compensation philosophies has been invaluable in her role as Compensation Committee Chair, and her diverse experiences in board leadership offer a singular guide for anyone who wants to 'Be Board Ready.'"

 - **Matt Maddox, CEO, WYNN RESORTS**

"Betsy's book will bring board candidates and members valuable insights and practical advice on how to participate actively and productively in the governance of a company. Betsy has the rare experience of having served on numerous boards across various sectors and geographies. Her book brings together her learnings from these diverse environments, supported by a hands-on and intimate knowledge of situations that board members have to navigate. An essential read when the governance of companies in the digital age is facing significant challenges, is undergoing major transformations, and requires different approaches in different parts of the world."

   - **Jean-Pascal Tricoire, Chairman & CEO, SCHNEIDER ELECTRIC**

"I believe Betsy Atkins's deep and broad experience of international board engagements should be very valuable to any board member or CEO."

   Håkan Samuelsson, CEO & President, VOLVO CARS

"Betsy's deep board experience is distilled into an action plan on how to join a board, be a valued colleague, and an asset for the business. Her coaching and wisdom is for CEO's, directors and teaches how to be a world class director and be prepared for what goes on in the boardroom. If you are involved in corporate governance it's a must read."

   - **Lone Fønss Schrøder, Vice Chairman of the Board of Directors, VOLVO CARS**

"Betsy's book helps new, prospective board members find a seat. She brings her philosophy of engaged, cognitive diversity on how to contribute in the boardroom into actionable steps for directors and CEOs."

   - **Robert Smith, Founder, Chairman & CEO, VISTA EQUITY PARTNERS**

"Joining a public Board can be a challenging experience even for the most seasoned business professional. Betsy has such a tremendous knowledge and experience from so many Boards that she draws from in this book to help you manage, enjoy and benefit from as you embark on the journey to be a Board professional. From personal experience with Betsy in the Volvo Cars Board I have learned a lot on how to manage Committees and work in the Board to maximize the benefit for the company, their business partners, their shareholders and importantly their employees"

   - **Tom Johnstone, Member of the Board of Directors, VOLVO CARS**

"Nasdaq has always valued best-in-class corporate governance and has partnered with Betsy for years as part of our Governance Clearinghouse, conferences, and in her role as a Nasdaq director. This book captures her insights not only on how to join a board but also on how to be a valued member. She provides terrific, practical advice that can benefit CEOs as well as current and future board directors."

- **Adena Friedman, President and CEO, NASDAQ**

"Betsy's book is a roadmap for how to join a board and then become a world class contributor. She distills decades of experience as a highly impactful board member into this practical guide."

- **Deven Parekh, Managing Director, INSIGHT PARTNERS**

TABLE OF

CONTENTS

INTRODUCTION

I was once contacted by a Harvard PhD student and was very surprised when she told me that I—as a member of over 20 different public boards—had served on the second-most boards of anyone in the country. As I reflected on it, I was surprised by the number of different situations I have been in and the different problems that I have had the opportunity to engage on and help solve.

This motivated me to capture my experiences in this book, which I was inspired to write for all of the people who are talented, capable, and deeply interested in learning about what goes on in the boardroom and in joining a corporate board.

Today more than ever, boards are opening the aperture of who they think is "board ready" to add thought diversity, gender diversity, global diversity, functional diversity, and generational diversity.

I wrote this book for aspiring directors who want to join a board for the first time and get some tips and insights on how to be a great director, contribute, and add value.

I think the role of the board has changed over time from traditional backward-looking oversight to an engaged asset to help move the business forward.

I have broken down the book into three sections. The first section of the book gives you a flavor for all of the different things you should do to create your personal brand, to position yourself to successfully land a board seat, and then to add value. The second section is on how to actually lead the board as either a chairman, lead director, or CEO, and how to get the most out of your board. The third section is a selection of some of my previously published articles that I've adapted for this book to illustrate some of the challenging and incredibly fascinating topics that come up in the boardroom that no one can teach you, that you have to experience for yourself.

My goal is to illuminate some of these topics and explain how I've seen them solved by participating on boards that address these subjects. I hope that these takeaways, learnings, and insights will be applicable to you as you go forward in your career, join your first board, or contribute further to the boards that are fortunate enough to have you serve on them.

SECTION 1

HOW TO GET ON A BOARD

CHAPTER 1

PERSONAL BRAND

DEVELOPING YOUR OWN BRAND AND PERSONAL POSITIONING IS A VERY IMPORTANT FIRST STEP IN THE PROCESS OF FINDING THE RIGHT BOARD FOR YOU.

FORMULATING AND COMMUNICATING YOUR PERSONAL BRAND

You should identify what you stand for as that is the basis for your personal brand. What are your key messages that you want someone to know about the value that you would add to a board and a company?

You will want to be crisp in distilling your career into three major digestible, thoughtful points. For example: What is your industry background? What is your functional expertise? What stage of company are you a best fit for?

My career background is as a serial CEO and entrepreneur and my experience and strengths are in developing start-up and/or established high-growth companies. So my strengths lean more to this kind of board opportunity rather than trying to apply myself to the turnaround of a failing business. This is my personal positioning, but you will need to think about your own and tailor it and be able to deliver your strengths in a concise way.

As you think about the unique essence of who you are as an executive, you will want to capture some of your distinguishing qualitative attributes. For ex-

HIGHLIGHT YOUR DIFFERENTIATING QUANTITATIVE AND QUALITATIVE ATTRIBUTES

ample: Are you an inspirational leader? Are you a visionary? Are you an amazing operator? Are you able to deal with global cultural issues? Are you able to pull together unique strategies? Figure out what are the qualitative experiences that are part of the core essence of who you are.

Quantitative attributes are more hard-coded, such as: Are you qualified as a financial expert and could you chair an audit committee? Have you had experience as a CEO running a company that went from $200 million to $1 billion in revenue? Or do you have healthcare sector experience?

These qualitative and quantitative attributes of your own "brand essence" are important so that you distill this in one or two short sound-bite sentences that are easily communicated and remembered so that as people meet you and come away from meeting you, they have a sense of not just your quantitative, measurable corporate experiences, but also your own personal attributes.

Here are some other things people will look for: Are you a consensus builder? Are you collegial? Are you a deep listener? Are you collaborative? Are you entrepreneurial? Are you innovative? These are some of the things that contribute to a board, along with some of your global work experiences, such as being effective at introducing innovation on a large scale in a global, long-established value company. Entrepreneurial innovation, or any other of your qualitative attributes, is likely to apply to every corporation, so having an example that you can explain succinctly and crisply will not only demonstrate your experience but will also show off your skills as a good communicator.

When you create your own brand, you should articulate your personal values in a discreet way as part of the thematic messaging that you want to continuously reinforce and emphasize.

You want to, essentially, be able to sound-bite your personal brand, who you are, what you stand for, and the value you bring.

Obviously, as each opportunity develops, you will want to customize your short-form bio and tailor it to a specific audience. That means researching carefully the company in question. You'll want to be able to talk about and apply your experiences that would be relevant to a company's industry and marketplace. Remember, the reason they are considering you as a director is that they expect you to provide oversight. But perhaps more important, they want you to add value and make the company more successful for its shareholders and target audiences.

GETTING THE WORD OUT THAT YOU WANT A BOARD SEAT

First of all, you need to think carefully about creating or refining your LinkedIn profile. You need to position your LinkedIn profile with a board role in mind and highlight experiences that would be relevant to a board, such as transforming a company, helping to grow a company, or restructuring a company.

You can maximize your LinkedIn profile by regularly posting blogs or articles to illustrate your knowledge and part in introducing and managing topical technological or corporate changes and developments.

For example, you may be able to post a blog about geographic expansion or helping companies enter emerging markets. Or you could communicate your role in creating high-value joint ventures. Or you might have been involved in identifying targets for acquisition or in driving through post-merger integration. These are all suitable case study examples, and there are many more where you can demonstrate your credentials to potential seekers of new board directors who can add value.

You might look at how you have reinvigorated a part of the business that had underperformed and how the work you've done has taken a stalled product or service and returned this stalled no-growth portion of the business to growth and reinvigoration. Be sure you consider carefully what you post on LinkedIn so that it links closely to your personal brand values that make you marketable to a board and/or is appropriate to board opportunities you may be targeting.

These are some of the predictable challenges companies and boards look to have addressed as something you might want to think about as the theme of what you're trying to communicate in the information you put on LinkedIn.

> SEEK OUT MEDIA EXPOSURE AND BECOME THAT GO-TO SUBJECT-MATTER EXPERT ON A TOPIC THAT TIES TO YOUR PERSONAL BRAND.

Additionally, you want to be able to be found in multiple online sites besides LinkedIn.

One of the ways that you will distinguish yourself is to consciously build a strategy on the media presence that you want to have and the key takeaway messages/slogans/themes that people should think of as a result of seeing, hearing, or watching your media content.

There is, of course, the social media and blogging, the writing of articles, the creation of video content, and the actual opportunity to do media in on-line Facebook webinars, YouTube, and, more important, TV media.

For example, this past year of 2018, I thought it would be valuable to create a media presence on the key business channels that my audience would be valuing, such as CNBC, Yahoo Finance, and Bloomberg. Within a year, I was able to have over ten meaningful air spots.

It's always a balance because you want to be able to display your thought leadership but be careful, very cognizant, and highly sensitive to the requirements of boardroom confidentiality. Any exposure always has a double-edged sword. You want to make sure that you are able to expose the integrity and unique value of your thoughts in displaying your business judgment and contribution as a board member but also be extraordinarily mindful of the requirement to respect the confidentiality of boardroom deliberations. This is a fine line that always must be observed. Always over-index on being more conscious of confidentiality in anything you say that could potentially be misread as a breach of observing the sanctity of boardroom deliberations.

Working with major media outlets, such as the *Wall Street Journal*, *Financial Times*, and other major business newspapers, is another way to build your media presence. Reaching out to the journalists who write pieces that relate to corporate governance is a way to build a contact base where you can offer to be either an on-the-record or an off-the-record resource as they write their articles. The more helpful you are to these major newspapers in creating content or providing background information, the more you will be well appreciated by the journalists; and over time they may see you as a go-to media expert once you build the relationship and demonstrate your willingness to help and be a resource for these journalists.

There are, of course, corporate governance online and print media publications, such as *Corporate Board Member*, *Directors and Boards*, *Directorship*, *Agenda*, etc. There are also adjacent publications, such as *Corporate Secretary*, *CFO* magazine, *CIO Journal*, etc. These are all media outlets that are tailored to the audience of public company directors or the people who conduct, lead and participate in corporate board meetings. Publishing in these outlets will again be a very direct outreach to a narrower and more specifically tailored corporate governance audience set. There is also the academic media—working with the corporate governance schools at Yale, Stanford, and Harvard, to name a few.

I have found it valuable to have an ongoing column in *Forbes* where I have the opportunity to write a weekly blog speaking about corporate governance. You want to define your swim lane and be narrow where your expertise is and very disciplined about opining, contributing, and creating a media reputation as an expert in a very specific, tailored, identified area where you feel you offer a unique viewpoint.

As you think about creating your media presence, it should be on a cohesive strategy that includes social media—written media for the community of corporate governance

You will want to consider if you have some original content that you could share that would be meaningful in your field or functional area or some experiences that you could write about, tweet about, or create and capture video content that would be relevant.

As you start to think about going on to a board, it would be ideal if you were currently still in your operating role. Being in your operating role gives you a great platform to tailor and build specific media exposure.

Think about which avenues are going to be the most comfortable for you and the most impactful. For example, you may want to start to think about what kind of content you can create with other people in your company while you are still in your operating role. Perhaps, for example, you are a business unit general manager or a functional organizational leader, such as in manufacturing or supply chain. Think about who you could co-author a piece with. Perhaps it's somebody from corporate strategy and business development. Come up with a theme and an idea that would be informative to other peers or peer companies. Develop a network of people who could be influential for you and would recognize and understand the insight that your content would provide and how that would apply to a board role.

For example, let's say you are a business unit general manager. Your head of corporate strategy and business development/MMA partners with you to acquire a company. How do you actually share your learnings on post-merger integration: extracting the value from the original company that you acquired; leveraging it effectively throughout your business unit; supporting cross-business unit leverage; globalizing and integrating this newly acquired entity to drive real value for the shareholders? A story like this—that you co-author with one of your colleagues at your current operating company—is a great way to create content.

Look at the content that other people in your role have created—other business unit general managers, or other functional roles, such as the CFO, chief strategy officer, chief marketing officer, chief manufacturing officer, and chief supply chain officer. Who do you read and where do you learn from? Do your homework and look at other general content out in the industry as sources for insights and learnings, such as McKinsey, Boston Consulting, Accenture, Gartner, etc. All of these are great repositories. There are also great business books that you may admire and may have learned from. Look at that content and see if you can extrapolate it, internalize it, and share an insight on how you use those learnings in your role. That's the kind of unique content that you could create that would be interesting.

You could then communicate this content as a blog, a tweet, an authored or co-authored piece, a comment that you make about other people's insights that help people see that not only are you current and contemporary in reading, but also that you can curate unique valuable insights from a large pool of information.

STAY RELEVANT AND VISIBLE ON SOCIAL MEDIA PLATFORMS. USE BOTH ORIGINAL AND SHARED CONTENT.

Becoming a curator or a bundler of insights is very valuable. Being able to consolidate useful information and giving proper attribution is always helpful for others and a good way for you to demonstrate your ability to digest, distill, and offer useful insight based on a variety of sources.

It doesn't have to be only content you create. Your value as an observer, digester, and curator of information is equally valuable as a way of showing how contemporary and thoughtful your views are.

Being regular and creating a cadence are important as you build your brand. Figure out the type of content you want to create or opine on. Give yourself a calendar of regularity and cadence of communicating. You can't create a brand with one or two touch points. It needs to be something regular. For example, it could be once a month or once a quarter but that would be minimum so that you create some body of work.

Another repository that you ought to research and mine is your company's video archives. Surely you have participated in a group or have been videoed at some point in your career. Take the time to find a video editor that you can engage to help create video content of you speaking in the company, speaking at conferences, participating in group discussions, or giving unique lectures at academic institutions or industry functions.

Create your video-content library. We are in the world of video content and you need to have content so that people can see what you look like; hear your voice; and get a sense of your personality, your authenticity, and your thinking and problem solving.

A couple years ago I hired a local videographer to capture the corporate governance mindset that I exemplify. We shot several segments covering a variety of topics. I created a schedule and posted these on my website and on YouTube. I had overwhelmingly positive feedback from the industry, and it provided several opportunities.

In parallel with your LinkedIn and your created content, you might want to think about creating your own website. Create a website that will be a repository for your written materials, video content, experiences, bio, and a gallery with some shots of you so that people can get to know you better.

THE CONTENT OF YOUR WEBSITE MUST SUPPORT YOUR BRAND.

There are a lot of easy-to-use website tools, and over time, you can refine and update your website on a regular basis. You will also want to link any video content to YouTube.

It's also important to look at where the future directions of your industry and experience are going. So, for example, if you're an expert in industrial automation, reading about the Industry 4.0 initiatives will be a valuable way of communicating how forward-thinking you are and talking about the various manufacturing innovations in quality and productivity.

If you are the chief human resource officer, having insight on how you engage with the gig economy, the shared economy, millennials, how you create a high-performing HR organization that could be applicable to a variety of corporate board situations would all be topics that you might want to try to get media exposure on, create your own content, and add to your LinkedIn, Twitter, a website, etc.

> **ALWAYS WRITE THE INTRO NOTE FOR THE PERSON INTRODUCING YOU. YOU WANT TO MAKE SURE THEY CONVEY YOUR VALUE.**

There are a variety of conferences that you should look into attending, participating in, and potentially being on a panel and contributing. By being active in conferences and giving speeches and presentations, you can communicate your experience, your expertise, your success, and the value that you're going to bring. Also, it's a way for you to meet a wide network of powerful people who could be helpful to you. You, hopefully, would be able to learn from them and contribute to their own learning. When you meet people at conferences, if you go out of your way to always follow up and follow through, you will distinguish yourself as the 1-in-100 person who actually does what they say.

KEY TAKE-AWAY

- Fine-tune your expertise and your differentiation.
- Develop a bio and always tailor it to your audience.
- Communicate branded content via:
    LinkedIn and other social media platforms
    TV, print and online media exposure
    Personal website
    Speeches and presentations

CHAPTER 2

BUSINESS DEVELOPMENT

IN ORDER TO GET ON THE RADAR OF A POTENTIAL BOARD, YOU NEED TO BE DISCIPLINED. YOUR PERSONAL NETWORK WILL GET YOU YOUR NEXT BOARD INTERVIEW, SO YOU NEED TO CARE FOR AND GROW YOUR RELATIONSHIPS.

EXPANDING AND MAKING THE MOST OF YOUR NETWORKS

Focus on attracting the attention of those who will be most influential and draw up a short list. To achieve this, you need to work at developing your own personal networks using some of the communications skills and platforms covered in chapter 1.

Your existing network is essential and needs constant attention to maximize the hidden potential it can provide. Consider all of the great executives and bosses that you worked with during your career that you admire. Look sideways within your own organization and develop networks with those younger smart colleagues you know who look like they may be the corporate superstars of tomorrow. Who are the current superstars where you work and on the senior executive leadership team? It would be well worth your while to reach out to these execs and cultivate the opportunity to sit with them for a quick espresso. A short reach out that talks about what you admired and have learned from them in the past year as you look forward in developing your own career is always well received. Most people within your organization, if you're explicit in your ask, will carve a little time out to meet with you. Alternatively, you can possibly cover such a conversation in your annual appraisal with your line boss if he/she is on your list of people you admire.

So, for example, let's say you really admire the chief revenue officer, who has expanded the company's business internationally, and you have an interest in international. As long as you are specific in your ask and are looking to get guidance on books and articles to read that have been meaningful as they have thought about growing their career, they would be generally receptive in carving out a very short slice of time. From this, you can build a relationship. This is just an example of how you build your network inside your corporation.

It is unusual to skip a level or go to a different functional organization. You need to be diplomatic and careful in how you make such an ask. It is normally well received, though, if you look at what they have achieved and

YOU NEED TO DO YOUR HOMEWORK BEFORE EVERY PERSONAL CONTACT. MAKE IT MEANINGFUL FOR BOTH OF YOU.

what you admire about them. Do some research on them. Go on LinkedIn and follow them. You can also comment on their blogs and build a rapport using online networking. Make note of the things they are good at that they seem to be really passionate about.

You should also go back to former bosses in your career as well and tell them how you have been progressing. Let them know what they taught you and how it has been meaningful in accelerating your own career. Mirror back to them the attributes in their leadership and in their success that you have most admired and tried to emulate. This will allow you to establish a good relationship looking backward as people will always ask for references, checking on you with former bosses, and you need to cultivate their enthusiastic support and approval. You can also ask them for guidance on your journey of who else they have admired and think you might learn from.

You have to be respectful and specific in what you want to get out of a conversation and keep it really short. Building a network is something that you do gradually over time. You invest in relationships. You have to remember you have to bring something of value to every meeting. You can't just go looking for people's time without earning credibility and respect that you are going to contribute to the conversation. You should have done some research about them and their areas of interest and be prepared to bring something that could be valuable and interesting to them. All relationships need to be symmetrical. You need to overweight on the forward investing as you cultivate and build a network so that they will be receptive to helping you down the line.

> DEVELOPING RELATIONSHIPS IS LIKE INVESTING MONEY IN A BANK. INVEST YOUR TIME AND DO SOMETHING THAT PROVES YOU ARE VALUABLE: GO OUT OF YOUR WAY, DO WORK FOR THEM, FOLLOW UP, DO THEM A FAVOR, MAKE INTRODUCTIONS, SHARE SOMETHING USEFUL AND MEANINGFUL. YOU MUST ACTUALLY ENGAGE. THE PAYBACK WILL BE GOODWILL AND SUPPORT FOR YOU IN RETURN.

Building a network is a continuous and long-term process. It's like building a campaign. Your goal may be a long-term project to get yourself on a board. It could be six months or more, even several years. Getting onto a board is rarely a one and done transaction. It's an investment in building relationships and you need to do the work to get there. This can involve doing favors and providing valuable information and useful insights. Your inputs can even help accelerate the career of the person you are targeting. So to come to a meeting "bearing gifts" in the form of intellectual capital you have spent time developing is always well received. This might also include an article, a comment, a conference to attend, a relevant book to read, or an introduction to a person who could be of benefit. All these things demonstrate your willingness to be helpful and thoughtful in developing a mutually beneficial business relationship.

By bringing something to the conversation, you are showing that you are not a taker, that you are a symmetrical relationship builder who will contribute back and be deeply appreciative of what they might have to offer you. I think that as you look at these things, you almost have to think of them as building respectful business friendships and relationships that can be essential in providing the openings and opportunities for board roles for you.

Forward investment is important so that those in your network feel proud to introduce you to others and those potential boardroom opportunities. In my experience the networks closest to you, with the people who believe in you, will be the ones that are the most likely key to help unlock that boardroom opportunity for you.

I advise attending a meeting with your network target with some prepared questions. People will enjoy meeting with you when they see that you are seeking their wisdom and their experience and that you are taking notes and paying attention, and that you follow up with an acknowledgment and a feedback loop to them.

Never underestimate the power and critical importance of closing the loop. People want to know they have been heard and have influence. People want the acknowledgment that you have absorbed the things they thought were valuable and that they shared with you. Taking notes is a way of saying to the person speaking that the content they are sharing is something that is deeply value and worthy of writing down. Review your notes,

BE SPECIFIC AND PLAN TO ELEVATE YOUR NETWORK SO THAT THEY MATCH YOUR OWN ASPIRATIONS. LOOK TO THOSE WHO CAN ENHANCE YOUR BOARD APPOINTMENT GOALS.

and then write a short follow-up that captures one or two insights that were unique and that are not just general thank-you language. Show you absorbed what they had to say and have taken note. It's always good to add a question or ask for a recommendation as the next step and have this be a way to build an ongoing relationship with them.

Creating a network in the place you work or have worked in, both vertically as well as horizontally, gives you a springboard for your own career development.

Apply this same technique to your other informal business circles. Ideally, you will have the opportunity to meet other networks that could be highly valuable to you. As you seek a board, one of the big influencers who interact with corporate boards is the investor community made up of both venture capital and private equity. You can also add the general council and outside law firms and accounting companies who advise the board, as well as management consulting organizations such as McKinsey, Boston Consulting Group, Bain, and Accenture. These are all valuable networks that you can cultivate. Try to build relationships in these different organizations where you feel you have a connection.

CREATE TAILORED TALKING POINTS

When you have the opportunity to pursue a live board position, create talking points tailored to the specific company. Is it an early stage company? A mid-stage company? A late-stage company? A public company? A growth company? A turn-around company? A value company? There are particular talking points that are relevant to the company's current status and future aspirations. Tailoring your experience and how it's relevant for the current status of the company is critical. It's not just a playback of your functional background or your industry background. You will need to demonstrate that you have the credentials and personality to help the board move the company from its current situation to where it wants to be.

Being able to weave in your values and your qualitative attributes, as well as your specific measurable industry and functional background, is essential especially when you get the chance—in baseball terminology, to "at bat" with key players in your quest for a board seat.

Typical at-bat opportunities are the chances to meet with a venture capitalist, a private equity person, a banker, a lawyer, a colleague, a prospective CEO, and/or a board member who could help you. These at-bat opportunities have to be carefully considered and prepared for. You may only have one chance to make a big impression. Come with your thoughts organized, prepared in an outline, and take full advantage of the opportunity.

Where possible, do your homework on the person you're going to meet. Understand who they are, their background, their values, and what would interest them. It is also worth trying to find a shared interest or common point of reference and mention it early in the conversation. This could be a host of things: born in the same city, attended the same college, support the same football team, have worked for the same company in the past, have mutual friends or business colleagues. Remember the old adage of "two degrees of separation" and usually you will find some common ground.

Match up what you would hope to contribute and where you would add value to their personal and professional journey and their areas of interest.

For example, you might have heard about a private company that is going to be building its board. You might say, "Do you think that the best way for me to approach this would be to try to find an access point to one of the investors or board members? Or do you think it would be a more beneficial approach to try to work through a search firm?" Another idea would be, "Do you think it would be my best approach to try to network with one of the senior executives reporting to the CEO as my best path in, or do you think I would be better served trying to network via their outside law firm that advises the board?"

These are examples of how you can think about getting access to a board opportunity. It also demonstrates when you go back to the person in your network who you think can be helpful to you that you are not coming empty-handed, that you're seeking advice and that you're looking for their wisdom on an actionable set of choices. This shows that you've taken initiative and done some thought. Nobody wants you to come and say, "Help me and do all the work for me, and I was too lazy to figure out some ideas on my own and I'm expecting you, my network/helpful person, to do the work for me." That's not a good way to approach things. People respond better when they see that you have actually done some work and you are seeking their advice on an actionable set of potential alternatives.

You want to be sure that you are not overwhelming somebody. A recitation of your life's resume and accomplishments will put people to sleep. Remember, in every conversation, as you're learning about the board, whether it's through search or bankers or lawyers or accountants or any of your business development resources, you want to be listening, and the discussion should be 70 percent them educating you on what's valuable and important.

You want to be careful to distill down to no more than three main specific points, three takeaway messages that focus on your capabilities. These capabilities can then be fed back to either the company or the people who might be introducing you to the company so that they can position you.

After the meeting, if they are prepared to recommend you, suggest that you provide the person, your promoter, with a brief summary of your attributes and rationale of why you are suited to the board position. He/she can then lift this "ghostwritten" information and may include it within his own submission to the company or headhunter in question. This not only makes the job easier for your promoter but it also ensures that nothing gets overlooked in his/her recommendation of you. It will also be appreciated by your promoter and be a demonstration of your professionalism for future opportunities.

In other words, you haven't asked them to do two favors for you, the first favor being the introduction. The second favor being, please do all the homework and write the letter! That's too big of an ask. Create a tailored version of your short-form bio and a ghostwritten note introducing you, and potentially leaving in the one or two, at maximum three, talking points or unique themes that are the sound-bites of the perspectives you're going to bring that are different from and complementary to the skills that are currently around the board table.

Talk to search firms and always take a recruiter's call, even if you love your current job. You may be able to

---

GET OUT THERE AND PRACTICE.

---

help them fill the slot by recommending someone even if it does not suit you. Now you have paid in and been helpful in case you need help in the future.

A very important avenue for finding potential board roles are the specialty turnaround consultancies such as Alvarez and Marcel, Alix Partners, BDO Seidman, and Buxbaum Group. Activist hedge fund investors are potentially great board opportunities for people who haven't yet served on public boards. The big activist funds are companies like Elliot, Carl Icahn, Third Point, ValueAct, Jana, Pershing Square, Starboard, and Trian.

TAKE ADVANTAGE OF THE PUSH FOR DIVERSITY

It is the moment in time, if you are a woman and you want to join a board, to really actively pursue this in a thoughtful, organized, programmatic way. There is a lot of research that you can do to figure out which boards need women appointees in its current composition. There is work you can do to understand which industries are best served by having more women representatives—for example, if it is a retail industry, where women make 70 percent of the buying decisions; or a hospitality industry, where women are big decision-makers; etc. So there are certain specific industries that will be more predisposed, while certain companies are laggards in adding gender diversity to their boards. Within the USA there remains significant geographical variations on this issue. Many countries have legal mandates they have to meet for women board members. For example, by 2020, in the UK 33 percent of the board and leadership roles must be female. Ask regional recruiters to introduce you to their European counterparts.

Women today have an incredible competitive advantage in trying to gain a board seat. If you look at the data from the Heidrick & Struggles board search practice, they stated that 37 percent, so over one-third, of every board seat they are filling for Fortune 500 companies is for a woman as a prerequisite.

That was as of 2017, and things have accelerated in a geometric fashion. The new proposed legislation coming out of California and New Jersey, as well as the actions of the big index funds mandating a minimum of two women, and soon a minimum of three on every board, is going to be a terrific positive catalyst.

Given all of this, there are additionally some terrific organizations that are dedicated to accelerating women into the boardroom. There are organizations such as The Athena Alliance, Trewstar, the 30% Club, and theBoardlist, to name just a few.

If you do your research, you will find that there are organizations that specifically will help as a conduit to opportunities where your background would be especially welcome.

Of course, you want to go with all of the other business development channels I've written about, including traditional executive search firms, marketplace search firms such as ExecRanks, bankers, attorneys, accountants, other colleagues, and mentors who could help you.

The specific attributes that you bring that would be especially prized as a woman board member often are in the finance industry. All boards are always looking to augment their audit committee. Other functional industry backgrounds that are being sought for board service are chief marketing officers, chief revenue officers, and women with supply chain and manufacturing backgrounds and engineering backgrounds are especially sought after. As you look at plotting your own career, if you haven't yet had a business unit general management position, this would be something for you to look at so that you will have the profit-and-loss ownership for a business unit or division, as general management is a particularly valuable perspective that is also sought after on boards.

YOUR FIRST BOARD OPPORTUNITY

When considering your first board opportunity, I would advise selecting a company where you have genuine interest and curiosity. Pick the ones you have a connection to. Ask yourself, "Do I like the CEO?" "Do I care about the business?" "Can I add value?" and "Am I going to accelerate their mission?"

Being selective is important if you want to make progress in your board career. Getting the first board right is the hardest. You need to be reasonable in your expectations and the likelihood is that you will achieve a private company board position before you earn your spurs to have the opportunity to join a public company board.

A word of advice is that, in my experience, sitting on a nonprofit company or charity board is not a great benefit as a stepping-stone to getting on private or public corporate profit-driven boards. They operate quite differently; and conversely, in my experience, you tend to get many offers to join major nonprofit boards and big charity boards once your name gets out there as a successful corporate board member.

For-profit corporate boards are a very different animal, and they are the first chance to prove that you are an asset and a valuable contributor on a future public board. Venture capital-backed, family corporate boards, and private equity boards are all for-profit corporate boards that will contribute to your knowledge, your learning, and your ability to prove yourself a valuable asset.

As mentioned earlier, getting your first board is the toughest, so you should work hard and accept the opportunities that you are able to develop. You need to get experience to prove yourself. Just because you join a board doesn't mean you have to stay for a life sentence. You can always rotate off as you get boards that are more interesting, more prestigious, more global, or boards that are public. You should not hold out forever waiting for the ideal opportunity; you need to prove yourself and get experience.

The same is true for a public board. Let's say that you are already serving on private corporate boards and now you are seeking your first public board opportunity. It would be very important to get a first public board in order to get a second or future public board. Many public boards have as a criteria for consideration that you have already served on another public board. This is a big first step and a critical one. Therefore, when you look at public boards that are available to you as a first-timer, it may not be a Fortune 500 company. It may be, for example, via an activist route. Or it may be an international board. Or it may be a turnaround board of a company that has stalled. It may not be that Google, Apple, Microsoft, and American Express are knocking on your door. You may have to prove yourself by having done work on other public corporate boards that had more challenging circumstances.

Activist hedge funds and turnaround consultancies are helping companies that are somewhat in distress or whose business has underperformed. This has caused a potential crisis in the boardroom where they have been pressured to refresh their board, either by an activist or by going through a difficult circumstance, such as an insolvency or a major turnaround. While these boards may not be your ideal board, they are great first boards. Having served on a public board is a distinct badge of recognition and honor. It is your ticket to ride to get to another public board. So, don't be too picky and standoffish in refusing to take a public board because it's not Exxon Mobile, American Express, or Proctor & Gamble. Go to a public board and pay your dues, and then from there use your colleagues on that public board as your new power network to cultivate.

Generally, most people who are serving on a board have served on one or more other boards either currently or in their past. Working with them and getting to know them is yet another network that you can cultivate. Your board members will always be something that future boards check with as part of their referencing on you. So, relationships with your board colleagues, the outside law firm, and the outside accounting firm are additional resources and networks for you to cultivate as you build your personal and professional future board network.

One of my first major public boards was a company I co-founded named Ascend. It went from $0 to $5.4 billion in revenue in about eight and a half years and was in the internet infrastructure equipment business. Ascend competed with Cisco and, subsequently, was acquired by Lucent Corporation. Lucent was a big, stand-alone telecommunications equipment company, and, unrelated to the fact that Lucent acquired Ascend, the board separately reached out to me and I had the opportunity to join the Lucent board, in crisis and learning. The company revenue went from $30 billion down to $8 billion in one year when the telecommunications industry imploded. Lucent had to go through a major layoff because you cannot support 145,000 employees that you have on the payroll when you are a $30 billion company a year later when you are an $8 billion company. There was major restructuring that was required and the company divested major business units, such as Avaya, the call-center business unit.

For me, having been a serial entrepreneur who came from high-growth/ hyper-growth tech companies that were highly innovative, joining a large telecommunications voice switch manufacturer was a shock. The product innovation cycle was seven years versus nine to twelve months. The company was very slow in its responsiveness. I found that it was not the ideal culture for me; I loved high-growth companies, so I used the Lucent experience as a springboard to move to another company named UTStarcom, which was a hyper-growth wireless base station telecom infrastructure manufacturer that was approximately a $6 billion company growing at 30 percent as opposed to a $30 billion company contracting 73 percent down to $8 billion. This was a better match for my skills at the time and I found that, while I learned an enormous amount about restructuring at Lucent, it was not something that was a core strength or area of passionate interest for me.

BE BOARD READY

The point being, you take the first high-profile opportunity that comes your way. You glean and learn. You use it as a stepping-stone to move to something that is a better fit for your passions and your experience and the areas where you feel you can make a more meaningful contribution.

KEY TAKE-AWAY

- Invest time in building your personal network.
- Make the most of at-bat meetings with influencers.
- Take advantage of search firms, turnaround consultants, and activists.
- Be opportunistic in seeking your first board appointment.

CHAPTER 3

BOARD INTERVIEW

PREPARING AND RESEARCHING IS THE KEY TO A SUCCESSFUL INTERVIEW.

INTERVIEW PREPARATION

When you think about how you prepare for a board interview, start by doing your research on the company and the other board members; research the marketplace through analyst reports; study the company from a financial point of view, how they are competitively positioned, and the trends in the industry.

AS PART OF YOUR PREPARATION FOR A BOARD, YOU SHOULD RESEARCH, EVALUATE AND MAKE AN ASSESSMENT OF THE CURRENT BOARD OF DIRECTORS.

Then create for yourself a matrix of the skill sets that are currently at the board table and identify any gaps that will help them grow and accelerate going forward. Are they missing a more global perspective? Are they missing different go-to-market methodologies and business models that you have experience with, such as a market place or an e-commerce web-centric go-to-market model? Are they missing detailed knowledge of mergers/acquisitions and integration?

Look at your own experiences and try to evaluate those around the table as best you can. You must ask yourself, "What is it specifically that I would bring?" How are you going to accelerate that particular business and add value? Think of three unique skill bullets that express why you are valuable and can make a difference. You cannot communicate more than that and they will not remember more!

> **DON'T WORRY ABOUT THE SKILLS YOU DON'T HAVE, FOCUS ON THE ONES YOU DO HAVE. THE INTERVIEW CONVERSATION SHOULD BE ABOUT THE COMPANY AND WHAT YOU CAN BRING.**

If you can't see a clear way that your experience is unique, different, complementary and additive, then it will be difficult for you to make a compelling case as to why you are a good fit for this board.

You should also research and understand where management says the company's growth and future are going to come from. Compare that to the current set of board members. And then analyze your own background, strengths, experiences and skills that could augment what is already present in the boardroom. Distill it down and make some talking points. These are the things that you would reference and weave into your conversation with either the search person or whoever is introducing you to the board, or in direct communication when you meet with or speak to the CEO.

You should have some clear messaging themes that you have made about your unique value that would be helpful, different and serve as an accelerant to this board as it goes forward.

For example, as I look at my own background as a serial CEO and tech entrepreneur, I think that the perspective I bring is a contemporary view on digital transformation and the use of technology to either accelerate the business and the customer journey using technology or perhaps in the back office use technology to take costs out of the business and increase efficiency. So I would look at a board and I might see that there are no board members who have a tech background and I would list the attributes in my experience that are different and additive.

Another important step in preparing for an interview is to problem solve the company's issues in advance and be able to articulate your thoughts on how to solve those issues.

- How can you help them grow and problem solve?
- What can you fix?
- What are their competitive dynamics?
- What issues is the company facing that you are worried about and how would you make them better?

One of the most valuable attributes that a management team, CEO and fellow board members will value in you is if you think like the CEO and you help the company and the CEO/board colleagues to problem solve some of the topics that the business faces.

Think about the competitive dynamics that the business faces. Try to offer useful insights, ideas, suggestions or questions that would help illuminate and create valuable discussion around the table on how the company could approach some of the challenges it faces or the opportunities that are in front of it. This is much better received than having an attitude of just asking for information and asking questions or identifying oversights and finding fault. Your attitude should be that of a helpful, thoughtful partner to the CEO and the board as you think about building the business, maximizing the opportunities, or addressing the challenges in a constructive way. That approach demonstrates your starting point and how you would offer such ideas to the CEO if appointed.

This is a very different attitude than just looking for information and not having prepared your thoughts. Challenging and probing in a constructive, gentle way with your board colleagues in this thought partnership approach is a really exciting positive boardroom dynamic.

In addition to your skill set, they are also looking to increase diverse members in their board to enhance the board's overall value to the company. They want to bring together different views from different experiences. You should look at the board's cognitive diversity, background diversity, diversity of experts in the company's industry, diversity of functional experts. It is also important to define diversity as diversity of thought, which is not just single-lens gender diversity. It is also ethnic diversity, geographic diversity, digital diversity, etc. Thought diversity makes for great discussions and decisions.

THOUGHT DIVERSITY MAKES FOR GREAT DISCUSSIONS AND GREAT DECISIONS.

Think about the diversity they are missing and how your background can help to fulfill it. Make them realize that your diverse background will help them see more opportunities and avoid risks.

Then you have to go the next level deeper and prepare by doing research on the CEO. Watch YouTube videos or read interviews of the CEO and senior leadership team. Pay attention to their jargon, their buzzwords, and what is important to their company culture. Doing that homework, studying that, and mirroring it back are critical because it will resonate with the person you're meeting with that you are able to use some of their favorite jargon and phraseology. Psychological mirroring can be helpful here.

THE INTERVIEW

I always do feel it is valuable and important to come to an interview with your paper and pen so that you can capture notes while they're fresh and points that are valuable. You don't want to sit through the interview making lots of notes, but you want to be able to capture something vital.

Remember, first impressions are vitally important. Your appearance and persona are actually hugely important. I recall earlier in my career going for a board interview and the woman who was the CEO was matronly. I came in in my most current outfit, which was perhaps a bit too short, a bit too provocative, and a bit too fashion-forward. I could tell within the first 15 seconds that I had failed the interview on my appearance alone. She looked at me and had hit the next button/eject. I just didn't look like what she wanted a board member in her boardroom to appear to be.

It didn't matter what my content was or the value I could have added. I just didn't look like her type of board member. You will want to do some studying on the company's corporate culture and how the other board members, the CEO and the leadership team appear and not inadvertently hit a tripwire that would eliminate you based on initial appearance.

An interview is a conversation that should be somewhat one sided—meaning, the interviewer should be talking two-thirds of the time. Your goal is to learn about them and connect with them so that when you share your experiences and qualifications they are interested in hearing about them.

Use specific examples to share your qualifications by telling a compelling story versus simply listing skills. Stories provide color and a view to your personality, which is very important in the boardroom. This makes you more relatable and likable.

Ask questions that are specific to the company, such as "What are some of the challenges that you are facing?" or "What skillset in the boardroom are you looking to fill?" These types of questions give you an opportunity to then discuss how you might be additive.

INTERVIEW FOLLOW-UP

Once you've exited the interview, you should, while it's fresh, write up the meeting notes. It's a very good discipline. Write up the whole scenario; write up the whole set of notes coming out of the meeting of what was

> FOLLOW-UP IS CRITICAL AND SHOULD CAPTURE WHAT YOU FELT WAS VALUABLE AND IMPORTANT TO THE CEO, NOT JUST WHAT YOU LEARNED.

discussed. What were the key insights from the CEO? What did the CEO think were the opportunities for the company going forward? What did the CEO think were the challenges? What did the CEO think were the competitive dynamics that the company would face as it grows? What were the priorities that they felt were important for the corporation and what was the profile of a board member that would be additive around the table?

Capture all your notes on that. Immediately, while it's fresh, do your rough draft of a follow-up note to the CEO. In your note, you will want to reflect what you understood the CEO believed were the most important insights. You will also want to make a connection to something in your experience that relates to what the CEO told you that could be helpful to the company as a board member in an area where you would be able to contribute value.

The follow-up should be short and it should be done within a day or so of the meeting so that your contribution stays fresh and in front of the CEO.

ANALYZING BOARD SEAT OFFERS

Once you have successfully secured a board seat offer, it is always a good idea to review all the details before formally accepting. You will only want to accept if you can commit to all the responsibilities and if it is a right fit for you.

First, you want to make sure you trust the CEO and believe in his or her vision for the company. Were there any red flags when researching the company, such as lawsuits or social media issues/crises? Did the board members seem independent or too clubby?

Through this evaluation process, try to be open and to absorb without prejudgments.

Of course, you want to make sure that you are able to give them 100 percent of your time. Make sure you review your calendar and other responsibilities. Make sure you not only have the time to attend board meetings but that you also have the time to be readily available and engaged should the CEO need your insights and recommendations.

After this evaluation, are you excited and feeling energized by joining?

Once you have made your decision, always be gracious, even if you are not going forward and you decline.

KEY TAKE-AWAY

- Do your homework and research their skills matrix.
- Present the three unique skills and diverse background advantages you bring to the company.
- Be a thought partner to problem solve prospective company issues.
- Research the CEO and other board members.
- Follow-up is critical.
- Analyze board seat offers before accepting.

CHAPTER 4

HOW TO BE A GOOD BOARD MEMBER

TO BE A GOOD BOARD MEMBER, THERE ARE SEVERAL COMPONENTS TO BEING EFFECTIVE AND A THOUGHTFUL CONTRIBUTOR.

BOARD MEETING PREPARATION

The first thing is your preparation. Of course, you need to read the materials that the company will supply you. This will be in the form of a board book that will cover all of the content of the agenda and the board meeting. There will likely be some committee work: compensation, audit, and governance being the normal three standing committees. You'll likely serve on one or two of those committees, so read your committee work carefully.

Additionally, you will want to self-educate; that is what makes a great board member. Look at financial analysts' reports. Get a copy of your CEO's report to the analysts from the quarterly report where the CEO has a recorded call with the financial analysts. Usually the chief financial officer and chief investor relations officer are on these calls. Listening to your CEO's quarterly recorded call is important. You ought to try to dial in to hear it live if you can. If you're not able to dial in and hear it live, get the transcript and read it.

There are also the actual analysts' reports from the various investment banks, such as Goldman Sachs, Morgan Stanley, JP Morgan, Barclays, and others, who track your company's stock and do write-ups coming out of the CEO's quarterly report; you should get those as well.

The bigger and more interesting thing, however, because board books and committee work are table stakes, is to be fully informed about the company's current status. You should read or listen to other industry insights about your company that exist out in the marketplace and compare how they stand against their competitors. Your company probably puts out a lot of information on their website and press releases that you ought to read. But additionally, look at the market research, not the financial analysts' research, but the market research on your company and your main competitors.

In the tech industry, for example, Gartner is one of the big research analysts. There will also be information from McKinsey, Bain, Boston Consulting Group, and from Accenture, who will publish information on your company's industry. Reading this research will give you a sense of the competitive dynamics; by the time you've ingested that, you'll be really well prepared.

Now comes the second big component.

ONE-ON-ONE MEETINGS

The second thing that makes a great board member is when you come to the board meeting. Try to book a little extra time to sit one-on-one with various members of the CEO's direct executive leadership team. It could be the chief financial officer one time, the general counsel, the chief revenue officer, the head of product, the head of manufacturing, etc., another time.

Now the key thing is to be sure of the protocol. You don't ever reach out to someone who works for the CEO without first clearing it and saying, "Would it be helpful?" "Would you mind?" "Would you be supportive if I was to spend a quick half-hour or an hour before our board meeting while I'm in town to meet with…?" and get the guidance and the approval from the CEO. It is a huge issue if you just directly reach out to anyone without clearing it.

Once you have that coffee with the CFO, be sure you write a short note to the CEO with the highlights of what you learned and what you discussed.

A cardinal rule, a red line never to cross, is that you are a board member; you are not an operating officer. You are not management. You cannot give homework or ask for requests or give priorities to anyone who works for the CEO. So, if you casually say to the CFO, "Hey, I'd like to see a cut on our numbers that shows how we compare with company ABC," then you're giving a priority in a work task. You can't do that. You might ask the CEO, "Would it be helpful if we examine the numbers comparing us to company ABC?" But you should never inadvertently give a priority or a task to somebody who does not report to you. That's what you put in the note to the CEO and it's his job then to act on it or not.

DURING THE BOARD MEETING

The next big part of how you comport yourself in the board meeting is the real place where the rubber meets the road. Are you going to be a good board member? Or are you going to be an annoying board member who adds no value?

It is not important for you to be heard and to speak often. Think of it like a baseball game. There are nine innings; how many times do you get at bat in a baseball game? You probably come up in the lineup three times. If you're a new board member, try to keep yourself to three comments, maybe five. Do not chime in to agree with people that's not moving the dialogue or conversation forward. Do not go way off topic in your questions—that will make people uncomfortable and it will seem like you're not following the main thrust of the conversation.

Be thoughtful in the three, maximum five, points you want to make. You want to be able to contribute useful insights. If you actually don't have anything useful to say, then you shouldn't be talking just for the sake of making yourself visible or known in the boardroom. Everybody sees that you are there.

It is absolutely reasonable to ask for clarification, and questions are good. It's also good if you have something that is going to move the conversation forward to contribute it, where there's a linkage. Since you've done all this prep that we talked about before, you will have great insights to contribute. You will likely be the best informed board member there because you will have done way more homework and you'll be way more current.

Also, by meeting with one or two members of the executive leadership team, you will learn so much in those one-on-one conversations that you will have amazingly valuable insight to contribute.

You were likely recruited to the board because you brought a specific background or skill set. For example, my background is as a tech entrepreneur, so I'm often recruited to the board as their digital director to think how tech can enable the product or service that the company offers. So it's logical that I make suggestions or present ideas for discussion along that topic. I am not, for example, the financial expert; so for me to ask a bunch of basic questions, I would only be displaying my lack of knowledge and slowing everyone down. If I have basic questions like that, I will go offline to the CFO either before or after the meeting. I'll make a list and get the basic clarifications.

The big mindset that you should have as your over-arching umbrella when you contribute and participate in the board dialogue is that you're there to be a competitive asset for this business; you are an accelerant. You should be there thinking as if you were the CEO: what are the challenges? You should be mentally problem solving about how the business goes forward, how it solves competitive dynamics, how it thinks about the risks that it may not have anticipated. Your role is to be a thought partner.

Additionally, your role is to stress test the logic in a constructive way; you're not there to be the fault-finder director. Everybody hates the person who points out the problems and the issues in a negative fault-finding way. You will cause people to be embarrassed and lose face, and people will cringe when you speak.

You want to be gentle in how you raise difficult topics. You need to learn how to disagree without ever being disagreeable. You should have a set of phrases that are your go-to phraseology when raising things, such as:

- Have you considered . . . ?
- What is your view on looking at this from a slightly different angle?
- May I have your permission to be controversial here and a little provocative?
- This is a great idea but have you considered what might potentially be some unintended consequences? What might those be?
- May we take an opposing view to think things through a little bit just to be sure we all have addressed all the issues as we reach our consensus and conclusion here?

That's the kind of language that is welcomed and won't alienate people.

If you really disagree with something and the board is pushing a decision and you are clearly not persuaded that the direction is correct, there are a couple of ways to handle this. For example, you might say things like:

- Might I have a little more time to reflect on this? I'm not quite there to make a decision yet. Would it be possible to come back very shortly?
- Could we possibly defer this for just a little bit more time to think it through? I know that there's time sensitivity here and I don't want to slow things down but I'd like just a small amount of additional time to digest this and ask my questions offline so that I don't slow the group down.

Board protocol is that the board wants to always be unanimous when they vote. It leaves a terrible, discoverable track record for the plaintiffs if the board ever has a split decision on a topic. The protocol is that the board simply won't vote on it or they'll take this subject off the table. You never want to ambush and surprise people by voting no or abstaining. Well before the vote is taken, you'll need to say, "I'm just not ready to vote on this yet."

Sometimes you need to look at the long game. Maybe you don't agree on something that the board wants to do but the majority has reached that decision. If you've had a chance to discuss it and air your thoughts, it's time to circle up, link arms, and adopt the majority decision as long as it isn't crossing the line of legality or integrity.

If it's a business decision and you don't agree with it, but the majority of the board has reached a consensus, then you have to just agree to agree and you have to go along with the group. You will polarize your relationship otherwise. Reaching a consensus is the nature of the board and that's its role. To discuss, debate and consider all sides of a topic before making decisions is what you are paid to do by the shareholders. You're not going to agree with everything. Sometimes you have to go with the majority and accept collective responsibility. Embrace it.

BOARD COLLEAGUE RELATIONSHIPS

Another important thing is building your collaborative relationships with your fellow board colleagues. Since you're the new person on the board, it's incumbent upon you to reach out. You should, over the course of the year, make sure you have a coffee or a phone call or a video conference one-on-one with each of your fellow board members. You want to learn their institutional memory. They've been there longer than you. They understand the business probably better than you. At a minimum, they have way more history and insights into the company's culture, the leadership style of the CEO, and the capabilities and qualities of the executive leadership team. They can also tell you the inter-board relationship dynamics among your colleagues. There is so much value to be gained by reaching out one-on-one to your board colleagues. They will admire, appreciate and respect you for seeking out their history and institutional memory. They will want to share this with you and you'll learn a lot. Also, in the future they'll be able to guide and advise you because they'll be invested in your success.

Reaching out will also extend your personal networks as mentioned in an earlier chapter. Many board members sit on more than one board, so they can be a source of future recommendations for you. So these are contacts well worth nurturing.

IN BETWEEN BOARD MEETINGS

Part of being a good board member is the work you do in between the board meetings: the time you spend, the engagement you give the company. You have to earn their trust and build your relationships. As you do this, the CEO and the CEO's executive leadership team will be welcoming and deeply appreciative of the time you invest in them in mentoring their leadership development skills.

One of the best ways to approach this is to look at your own career and see where your functional domain strengths and expertise are. For example, if your deep early DNA as a functional leader was in product development, then the natural people for you to mentor would be on the innovation product development side of the organization, as opposed to the manufacturing or the finance team. If your early functional executive leadership/operating experience was as a CFO, then the logical area you would do your mentoring would be with the finance organization.

One of the ways I like to mentor leadership teams is on how to build a global go-to market organization, how to layer in the partnering and ecosystem relationships, and how to hire and build the team for the different phases the company is going through. Help the CEO and the other portions of the executive leadership team as they think about these types of strategic topics. First I ask the CEO if it would be helpful to her or him for me to build a closer relationship with one or two members of the executive leadership team to do ongoing regular touchpoint mentoring and building of their leadership development skills. Even if the CEO isn't ready yet for you to do this, they will be genuinely touched by your sincere offer to spend your time in helping the CEO develop the skills on the team.

Another kind of mentoring that you can offer to do can coincide with your quarterly board meetings. I do this, for example, at Volvo, where I offer to host a women's executive leadership lunch a couple of times a year. I meet with the middle management and top management—and even some of the line management women leaders from the factory floor—to talk about how they can build their careers, how they can take ownership for charting their own goals and paths, and how they can identify for themselves the types of skills they will need to develop to be successful. I like to have the opportunity to be exposed to and understand the company's culture, the priorities, and the topics these women leaders are concerned with. The HR organization and the other functional organizations have found this to be helpful.

This is the kind of mentoring that you do with a larger group, which is very different from building a closer relationship with one or two of the executive leadership team members to help them on their career path; very often it is the CEO herself/himself with whom you are doing the direct mentoring.

If you adopt some or hopefully most of these suggestions, you will become the most admired and esteemed colleague in the boardroom. You will have been seen by your colleagues to be prepared, thorough, professional, thoughtful, open-minded, a deep listener, and able to add value and contribute.

Your board colleagues are a huge source of reference checking and recommendations to new board opportunities. People will always be able to figure out who you served with on the board. They will always check with some of those people. If even one of those people thinks you're a jerk, it could sink your new board opportunity. You may not love everyone, but by seeking them out and listening to them, you will build a level of respect and of professional camaraderie that will serve you well as you go forward in your board career.

KEY TAKE-AWAY

- Prepare.
    Read your board package and committee work.
    Educate yourself on the company, its competitors, and the industry through company reports and analyst reports.
- Once encouraged, meet with the CEO's executive team.
- Be strategic and valuable during board meetings.
- Collaborate and build relationships with board colleagues.
- Mentor within the company.

CEOS AND FOUNDERS— HOW TO BUILD, EFFECTIVELY MANAGE, AND MAKE THE BEST USE OF YOUR BOARD

CHAPTER 5

THE ROLE OF THE BOARD

UNDERSTANDING THE ROLE OF THE BOARD AND GUIDING IT ARE KEYS TO SUCCESSFULLY LEVERAGING IT AS AN ASSET AND AN ACCELERANT FOR YOUR COMPANY.

RULES OF ENGAGEMENT

Set the ground rules of engagement early so that everyone on the board understands their role. It is just like a family table. They're your family; they're your investor family. An early step is to teach board members the difference between oversight and overstepping. Board members often don't understand what qualifies as oversight or an overstep, so you have to really

> **THE FIRST THING BOARD MEMBERS SHOULD DO IS TO TAKE THE GOVERNANCE HIPPOCRATIC OATH TO "DO NO HARM" TO THE COMPANY.**

spend some time training them that they are there to provide input and strategic guidance, not to overstep. So to get value, train them early on how to engage and be thoughtful and helpful. Guide your board on the right level of engagement and use your chairman or lead director to assist and share feedback when board members are overstepping.

Here is the thing: board members come to play. If they are going to contribute their knowledge, they have to feel that their psychological, ego and emotional paycheck is being fulfilled. And if you, as the CEO, don't give them things to engage in, they're going to be impossible to manage; it's going to be a tangential meeting that zigs and zags and goes everywhere. It's incumbent upon you, as the founder, to figure out the value your board members can bring. Challenge them to do the mental exercise of where they are most helpful to you, not just individually but also throughout the firm and throughout their portfolio of companies, and get them thinking that way on the front end—that they're not there to be a sharpshooter and lob grenades into the boardroom. They're there to actually add value and to be engaging, and that is their mission. You need to say, "I'm a smart, capable person; look what I've achieved. Now you can be an accelerant to my business; you can be an asset. How can you most add value? Let me understand where you can be most helpful to me." And if you get them thinking that way, then you're training them at the front end to lean in to be helpful, not to be fault-finders.

Listen to all views in the boardroom, but the CEO and management should be coming to the board with a recommendation for the board to provide feedback and input. Major decisions must originate with the CEO/management.

KEY TAKE-AWAY

- Set the ground rules for your board's engagement early.
- Specifically tell them where you want input each meeting.
- Challenge them to add value and assign specific tasks to accelerate the business.

CHAPTER 6

BUILDING A BOARD

CREATE A MATRIX OF SKILLS THAT YOUR COMPANY WILL NEED TO TAKE YOU THROUGH THE NEXT 5-7 YEARS AND FILL YOUR BOARD WITH MEMBERS WHO MEET AND EXCEED THOSE DESIRED SKILL SETS.

UNDERSTAND YOUR COMPANY'S NEEDS

The first step is to figure out what you need. Think about the functional capabilities and expertise that will accelerate the business and then try to map that to the attributes of board members who bring different and complementary perspectives to the discussion.

It is extremely important for CEOs to look at potential board members' profiles and define the ones who have previously been through a company journey from ideation to the birth canal. Take note of the ones who have been there from the start of the company's business plans and the ones who have experience in companies that have grown from the first $5 million to $15 million to $100 million.

CEOs are also going to forward hire board members. Just as CEOs and founders outgrow their executive teams, and they hire positions such as a new head of engineering, a new CMO, so too they outgrow some of their original team. A company is expected to go through maybe two or three sets of executives from $0 to $100 million.

The same is true of the board; they need to forward hire members. From the beginning, it is important to stress, and for board members to understand, that although they have their rights, and their seat, you're going to have a governance process that lists the skill sets and profiles of prospective members.

A company will need board members, or two or three board members, with experience that is well matched to the organization's current and upcoming stages of growth. Companies may want to have a sitting or former CEO among the mix. Companies should also look for one or two people with deep domain expertise who understand their business.

They will want at least one or two members who either come from that specific industry or have been in related, adjacent industries with customers that are similar to the ones they are targeting. And every company needs at least one board member with digitization, digital transformation, or technology expertise. Pretty much every business today is going through a digital transformation of some kind and needs to understand how to monetize their big data through analytics and to implement distributed global computing and secure mobile access, whether it is doing business by e-commerce or using e-commerce to take costs out of the supply chain.

DIVERSITY IN THE BOARDROOM

CEOs also need to look at cognitive diversity in their board members: how people think differently and problem solve differently. Diversity should also include diversity of backgrounds in the boardroom, diversity of domain experts in the company's industry, and diversity of functional experts, such as financial experts for audit committee, digital experts, and geographic diversity. It should not simply be gender or race diversity.

They also need to manage diversity by really looking into their board composition and thinking about how to hire the optimal set of differentiated and complementary perspectives required for effective oversight. The board should be an asset that the CEO and management can leverage to help stress test future plans as well as per-

> **DIVERSITY IS: COGNITIVE AGE DOMAIN EXPERTISE FUNCTIONAL GENDER ETHNIC GEOGRAPHIC**

form broad oversight for current plans. Just as management refreshes their leadership team frequently, so too the board should be refreshed to meet the challenges and opportunities the company will face during the next five to seven years, given the velocity of change.

BOARD COMMITTEES

When you think about creating a board, there are specific roles and responsibilities that are required. Typically for a public company, there are three committees: (1) the audit committee, (2) the compensation committee, and (3) the nominating and governance committee.

Even with a private board, it's a good discipline to add an audit committee and at least a compensation committee while still private. This will help the management and leadership team to get the perspective of operating executives, not just the perspective

> **THE THREE MAIN BOARD COMMITTEES:**
>
> - Audit
> - Compensation
> - Nominating & Governance

of investor board members who at some level may potentially be conflicted since they may be incentivized, for example, to minimize dilution versus the market competitive dynamics to have a big enough equity grant to attract key individuals.

The key responsibility of the audit committee is to be sure there are appropriate financial controls, internal controls, to mitigate risk and to assure the shareholders that information that is reported is reliable, has been reviewed by the appropriate independent auditors, complies with Sarbanes-Oxley, and gives information that people can confidently rely on for buying and selling decisions.

It is my own personal preference that the audit chair be a former or current chief financial officer. An operating executive will have a slightly different set of skills and insights than that of a former audit partner. An audit partner will have very good insight on internal financial controls complying with Sarbanes-Oxley but may not have insight, for example, regarding the nuances of messaging quarterly results, the scar tissue and pattern recognition for how to set expectations with the major shareholders, how to deal with the nuances of messaging a quarterly miss or a quarterly overachievement, and the ability to coach the team from an investor relations' perspective so that expectations don't get too far out in front of the company. Also, of course, a former CFO or current CFO will have a lot of valuable insights on the treasury functions, on currency fluctuations, and on complex financial instruments the company may want to utilize.

For a compensation chair, a really good background is somebody who has been an operating executive and is aligned with management on the importance of having a compensation structure that has a clear bonus that drives the results and performance that management wants the company to achieve. I prefer compensation chairs who favor simple compensation structures where the three elements—base salary, bonus, and long-term incentives—are clearly articulated so that the leadership team can understand and absorb the plan and is motivated by the plan. Overly complex plans often result in the opposite of the intended motivational effect.

For the nominating and governance chair, one of the key things is someone who understands the issues of tone at the top and the importance of having policies and programs that create a culture that is vibrant, that attracts all demographics (millennials, Gen X and Y, boomers), that is global in values and mission, and that is able to build a board and continuously refresh the board for the company's next leg of the journey. Also, a governance chair should have been through some of the difficult, complex, challenging issues in their career that might necessitate the creation of a special committee and must understand the nuances of what a special committee's scope is so that they're able to oversee special committees, should that be required.

In all three standing committees—audit, compensation, nominating and governance—you will want to have chairs who have served on committees at least once or twice before. You don't want someone to chair a committee who has never really had multiple different experiences serving on the committee. Preferably, especially for audit chair where you can, it is good to have someone who has already been an audit chair.

MANAGING YOUR BOARD

For an early, young entrepreneur or CEO who has to set up their board and may be intimidated, especially since their board is likely made up of investors, it can be helpful to recruit an ally board member who has the intestinal fortitude to guide/rein in investor board members. Each board needs one director who is the firmest member and can collegially give feedback to other members. This "quarterback director" can disagree without being disagreeable and say the hard things to difficult board members. Use this person to drive consensus and keep your board focused on building the business. Remember that even though you have investors on your board, they need to fit in and add value. Don't just pick an investment firm when you take in capital; choose which partner you have rapport with and select them for your board. Ensure that you have input in additional independent board members who are filling in the gaps in the matrix of skills you need around the table.

The single most important take away is for a CEO to learn to manage the board and get value from them. If you do not manage them, they'll manage you and you will always be defensive. What happens then is that you end up with these weird and unhelpful behavior patterns. Next thing you know, you will look around the table, everybody will be sitting in their same place, and they will have assumed their own self-appointed role: "I'm the brilliant hypothesis person," "I'm the provocateur who challenges all the logic," "I'm the smartest person in the room, who has to show off," "I'm the helpful supporter, the cheerleader." So you end up in these weird roles, and people can't get out of the roles—just like they get agitated if someone oversteps and sits in their board seat because they want to sit in the same seat.

For the founder CEO: what you want to do before you start the meeting is to have a conversation about the help you want and the role of the board. If you actually talk about it and express where you want their engagement and where you think they will add value, you will focus their efforts in the most helpful areas.

For Vista, I created a concept of a scorecard that included mutually identified deliverables for the company board members.

For companies that are now early stage, as low as $15 million, what you do as the CEO is to talk with the director and ask, "Where are you the strongest? Where do you believe you can add the most value?"

And let's say I'm the CEO of a healthcare company. I know that you have a background in healthcare, so I say, "I really need your industry knowledge. This is really helpful for me to augment my team because you were a physician and had a physician practice company in your past, and we do physician practice software. So your knowledge of physician practice organizations is really helpful."

So find an area where you think your board member can be valuable. And if they're just a junior finance guy, then look at their colleagues and say, "You could bring me access to your partner or your managing director. And by the way, you have this portfolio of companies. It would be helpful for me if you invited one of your CEOs to have a working dinner on how they did the customer journey, because they are a direct-to-consumer company, and I'm a B2B company, but I want to learn the customer journey that took the friction and the pain points out for a consumer company and adapt it to how I engage with my B2B, go-to-market channel."

KEY TAKE-AWAY

- Board members' skills should align with a company's stage of growth, include industry knowledge, embrace digital transformation, and possess the functional expertise required for the board to provide oversight.
- CEOs must lead and manage their board, no matter what stage they are in their growth.

CHAPTER 7

BOARD MEETINGS

THE BOARD MEETING IS THE CULMINATION OF A SERIES OF COMMUNICATIONS THAT SET THE TONE FOR THE IN-PERSON MEETING WHERE YOU AS CEO CAN ENGAGE YOUR BOARD TO STRATEGIZE AND HELP YOU ACCELERATE YOUR COMPANY.

BEFORE THE BOARD MEETING

I think that as a young CEO, managing your board and your board meetings to get value is something that you can do really well—or you can end up falling back on your heels.

As you begin to plan your board meeting, make it a part of your standard cadence to **telephone** each board member a week or so before the board meeting. These calls don't have to go too deep; they can be brief 10-minute calls just to see what issues or topics are on their minds. This way, if a board member has a big concern, you have the opportunity to diffuse it rather than be ambushed in the meeting. You are far better suited to get their input and create an agenda that they've given input on.

Write **a letter to the board** a few days before the board meeting crystallizing your thoughts and their thoughts. Communication to the board about your agenda is important. This also helps focus the board on the key points. This will get them thinking that you have your act together. This should be a two-page letter that speaks to:

- What you're going to cover
- What you've accomplished
- The challenges you're thinking about
- Your desire for input, engagement and guidance on these specific things

If you don't give them one or two meaty subjects to engage on, then it will be a frustrating board meeting, you will lose control, and they'll engage on a bunch of tangential stuff that won't be helpful to you and will drag you down rabbit holes.

SETTING THE TONE

- 10-minute call to each board member before meeting
- 2-page overview letter to board
- State of the union address at board meeting
- Board package that's concise with action items and information clearly stated and key takeaways and conclusions called out
- Assign "asks" to the board and make a follow-up list

THE MEETING

At the beginning of every meeting, just like the president of the United States does the **State of the Union** once a year, the CEO should do an overview of what is going to be covered. It should be a 15 to 20-minute summary.

Then the CEO should go through the information in the **board package**. Do not dump on the board a 250-page board package—which everybody gets cranky about. It should be no more than 35 pages with attachments.

Explain to your board that at the top right of every page, it should say "Information" or "Action" and at the bottom of each page it should have a conclusion or "Takeaway." Board packages should be provided at least three days in advance of the board meeting.

FOLLOW-UP

The other thing you should do in all board meetings is to have some administrator, whether it's the General Counsel, the Corporate Secretary, or somebody, taking notes and actions for follow-up. Some board members will always volunteer in the enthusiasm of the moment—"Oh, I'll make that intro" or "I'll do this"—but then they follow up on zero. And so you capture that and give them assignments. They're much more manageable when you give them homework and tasks. Then they stop bothering you. Because they're going to consume your cycles if you don't consume theirs. An email should go out after the meeting with the follow-ups and actions items and who they belong to. This should be separate from the board minutes that are sent out for approval. These are action items that are to be followed up on.

All public companies have an executive session where the independent board members meet alone without the CEO or any other company affiliates. This is an excellent practice for private companies as well. Support your board's executive session. This is the time when the board can candidly discuss company strategy and assess leadership. The lead director or chairman should head these meetings and ensure that everyone has a voice. He or she should then consolidate the feedback and report back to the CEO. Listen and learn from your board; you can't think you have maximized your potential, because surely you haven't. Target your strongest players on the board, understand their strengths, and use them for them strengths. Who is your finance person? Who is your tech person? Who is your leadership person? Build a rapport so that they can be your advisor at any time.

KEY TAKE-AWAY

- Setting the tone before the board meeting will serve to keep your board informed and focused on the key strategic decisions that you require their input on.
- Bring up problems and socialize ahead of the meeting.
- You want your board meeting to be an engaged, strategic collaboration rather than a review of what has already happened.
- Have someone taking notes during the meeting to capture follow-ups and "asks" for board members.

CHAPTER 8

BOARD REFRESHMENT

YOUR LONGEVITY AS CEO IS DIRECTLY TIED TO YOUR BOARD. IF YOU HAVEN'T SELECTED AT LEAST ONE-THIRD OF YOUR BOARD WITHIN 18 MONTHS, STATISTICALLY YOUR TERM WILL BE LESS THAN FIVE YEARS.

BOARD TERM LIMITS

As a CEO, it is important to manage and limit board members' length of service on the board. Put into place processes such as annual elections and term limits that allow you to rotate members and systematically review and assess the skills and gaps.

Early stage companies put in place an audit committee and a compensation committee. What they don't always put in place is a governance committee. If you're an early stage founder and CEO, you can tell the board, of course, that you are going to have a compensation committee because investors want to control equity dilution. And, yes, you are going to have an

BOARD STRUCTURE BEST PRACTICES

TERM LIMITS
EMPOWER ALL THREE COMMITTEES
ENGAGE AND EDUCATE
ANNUAL ASSESSMENTS

audit committee because you want to do the 409(a) valuation to raise the stock value. So you have those things, but you're going to have a governance committee too because this is an asset. If they don't really know what to do because they don't know much about governance because they are early stage investors, then you can lead them and you can have something different from what everybody else has.

Once you have a governance committee, you can put into your governance principles that the role of the lead director or chairman auto-sunsets each year. A typical term for a lead/chair is often five to seven years; however, if you were to get sideways with this key board leader, you need a mechanism in place that enables you to remedy this.

You'll want to keep your board engaged and educated. You can have two working dinners a year. Instead of going out to a restaurant, have the board stay in the meeting room and bring in pizza and salad; have some outside speakers, futurists, someone from the National Association of Corporate Directors; have somebody from the index fund Vanguard share what they think of corporate governance; have somebody from Institutional Shareholder Services talk about proxy voting recommendations. Have somebody like me who speaks on corporate governance, and train them to be an asset. They've never heard this. They actually do want to do a good job. You'll train and encourage and funnel them. You will get a better outcome.

And the miscreants who behave badly will at least have heard it discussed enough times so that, by the third or fourth year, when it's time to rotate them because you've outgrown them and they're painful, it will not be a total surprise. And it's easier; it's not like ripping the Band-Aid off. They accept that maybe it's time to do a forward hire on the board.

Implement a process so that the task for board refreshment is expected and a standard part of the board's annual self-assessment.

a. Task your governance chair to refresh half the directors each year for the next 3-5 year journey of the company.

b. Perform annual reviews with the board and include the performance that you are looking for from the board—something along the lines of "Here's what we hope to get from this board this year. We think you could be really helpful with this part of our growth strategy. Should we go to Latin America or the Middle East?" Or "Help us by mentoring these three executives who I think have high promise." Whatever it might be, come up with something where they can provide guidance and help.

c. Have the conversation, as a CEO, once a year, so that the board hears you being accountable for contributing and performing. That's a new thing, a new message for them. And if you say that the first year, they sort of blow it off. The second year, they hear a little murmur. The third year, they actually digest the content. And by the fourth year, maybe you can get them to be more constructive.

So I think the advice for how to get value out of your board and how to rotate your board that you've outgrown is to implement processes that constantly reinforce the idea that board members are expected to contribute tangibly to the company and that they will be assessed annually to determine if they fit the skills matrix that the company needs at that moment in their journey.

ROGUE DIRECTORS

Boards have personalities. They can be open, interactive, engaged, formal, command-and-control environments. Obviously, there are many shades of gray in between, but these predominant board personalities can be significantly impacted by a rogue director.

The problem of a director becoming a rogue who takes on too much power, authority and decision making, or becomes loquacious, disruptive or argumentative is significantly worsened and exacerbated in a command-and-control board environment.

Open, engaged board environments are fostered when the lead director makes sure that each member of the board can participate, is heard, and can actively contribute. When all members participate, you create a bonding or a "processing as a team," and this positive peer pressure keeps any single member from going rogue.

When a colleague goes rogue, it really is the responsibility of the lead director or governance chair to invest the time to have a series of discussions to help that colleague modify their negative behavior. There needs to be time invested to gradually bring this colleague back into a productive behavior mode. This can only be accomplished by investing the time to build enough of a trusted communication and rapport to help reshape the negative behavior. This is also an opportunity to engage your quarterback director, if you have been able to add one to your board.

Ultimately, if the rogue director can't be modified, then it may be necessary to ask that director to not stand for re-election. It is important when delivering the message that a director is not going to be invited to stand to try to shape this in a way that preserves the rogue directors "face" and dignity. Be as gracious as possible in representing the company's deep appreciation for their past service. When delivering the message that a director will not be invited to stand, it is essential that this be presented as an absolute conclusion so that there is no misunderstanding and to minimize awkwardness. This past director will remain connected out in the industry, so it is important to do preventive damage control for the company's reputation and so that this transition be as smooth as possible.

Dealing with a rogue board member or communicating to a board member that you do not want them to stand for re-election is one of the hardest things you have to do on occasion as either a governance committee member or governance chair. Typically, it falls to the chairman, the non-exec chairman, the leader director, or the governance chair to be the one who works with a rogue or who has to inform someone that they're not going to stand.

Many years ago on a board I served on as lead director, I had to tell two extraordinarily qualified, very capable, iconic, nationally recognized former CEOs that we were not going to go forward with them on the subsequent year's nominating slate. The reason here was that the company thought they might go in one direction from being a business-to-business company to a business-to-consumer company. Because the company changed direction and concluded that they were not going to go direct to the consumer, we no longer needed these iconic CEOs who had huge domain insight and knowledge on retail and branding.

Obviously, everyone who is a board member is highly accomplished. They generally would be bruised and would have their feelings hurt if they were not invited to serve and stand. The best way to do this is to actually go in person and sit privately a couple of times in advance to inform the director that there's going to be a shift in company direction, that their background and experience won't be needed going forward. Be sure to express deep appreciation for and acknowledgment of their service, and that this is not a reflection on their career or capabilities.

With a rogue board member, my experience has been slightly different. I have served as lead director where we had a very difficult rogue director who was brilliant, had great insights, but was disruptive and caused much collateral damage. Every meeting we would have an executive who would be attacked during the presentation so that the board dynamics were shut down and it was always a deep worry that we would have a key executive bruised and might even consider departing the company. The value of the board member was great in terms of their domain knowledge and insights. Their delivery was difficult. The only way to deal in this situation was to invest the time and spend time in person to build a direct rapport and relationship with the rogue board member. Gentle and continuous coaching before and after the board meetings was the only way to change the behavior.

These are all extraordinarily accomplished people. A rogue often has a big ego and isn't able to self-monitor and be self-aware of how their speaking and delivery are impacting other people. Because they aren't especially self-aware, the best way to handle this is actually to speak and meet just prior to a board meeting and sync up with the rogue and help guide them to where they will be most valuable and where their ideas and contributions will have a positive impact. Also explaining how they inadvertently are bruising other people or having a negative impact on others is an important part and is most effective pre-meeting. Once you know you have a rogue, they are likely going to continue to be a rogue, and it's very hard for people to change behavior. The best way is to speak to them right before the meeting.

If your rogue director is somebody who clings too long to an idea and argues too strongly for her or his point of view, again, I think you need to speak with them before the meeting. Let them know that their idea is in the minority. Tell them they will have their opportunity to make their case. But speak with them specifically and discuss with them the fact that they're going to have the opportunity to speak, debate, disagree, but in the end the board is going to make a decision and they need to commit. They cannot continuously reopen a topic or retread a collective decision.

Again, these topics have to be done in private, one-on-one, and are most effectively done right before a board meeting—sometimes after a board meeting, but after a board meeting the damage is already done. Once you know who your colleague is and what their behavioral aberrations are, you're best suited to tackle it just before a board meeting. It is generally most impactful that way rather than after the meeting when the damage is done.

KEY TAKE-AWAY

- Expect your board to contribute and tailor/specify where they can be most valuable.
- Create all three committees and set the precedent that each year members will be assessed for fit and the needs of the company going forward.

CHAPTER 9

NEW CEOS & BOARD RELATIONSHIPS

YOU CAN'T BE AFRAID OF YOUR BOARD AND AFRAID TO CHALLENGE THEM. IF YOU ARE, THEN YOU ARE ALREADY VULNERABLE. BUILD RELATIONSHIPS WITH YOUR BOARD LEADERS. BRING THEM INTO YOUR CIRCLE AND THEY WILL BECOME SUPPORTERS.

PUBLIC COMPANIES

In a public company, when a new CEO comes in, the statistics are that two-thirds of the time you promote from within. And additionally, the actual success rate tends to be higher from internal promotions. If you're an internal promotion, it will be easier and more natural for you to already have relationships with the board because you likely will have been a known successor who presented in board meetings with some regularity.

If early entrepreneurs and CEOs don't have strength, they end up getting replaced. You have to build up your courage and fortitude. If you want to be the long-term leader and not end up being the first leader, the second or the third leader, then you want to actually be the leader. If you want to be the Steve Jobs, the Bill Gates, if you want to take the journey, then you have to own the board as an asset and a resource. And you have to lead them and get value from them. They are expensive in terms of your time and your psychic energy if you let them go awry. They will eat you up; they'll replace you. It will be a lot of extra work and wasted energy in managing them, so you should engage with them and lead them. And if you do that proactively, it's way better.

> **THE KEY THING FOR YOU TO DO IS TO ESTABLISH DIRECT PERSONAL RELATIONSHIPS WITH EACH OF THE BOARD MEMBERS. EVEN MORE IMPORTANT IS FOR YOU TO ASSESS THE POWER DYNAMIC IN THE BOARDROOM.**

There is always the rule of one-third, one-third, one-third. What I mean by this is that one-third of the people on the board are the leaders. They're the thought leaders; they're the influential people whom the other two-thirds of the board follow. Then there is the middle third; they pretty much follow and they are the group that you have to get some support from. The bottom third are the naysayers, the skeptics, and the people who are generally less helpful. These are the board members who are disengaged and not highly effective. They tend to be quiet; or in a bad scenario, they tend to be the negative, opposing board members.

The key for you will be to establish a relationship with that first third. They are most likely the committee chairs, your chairman of the board or your lead independent director, your head of audit, your chair of compensation, and your chair of nominating and governance. Those four people are usually the most influential and they are the people who will actually end up deciding your fate—if you succeed and stay, or if they lose confidence in you.

If you build a really strong and solid relationship with your committee chairs and your lead independent or chairman of the board, you'll be in good shape. If you are not regularly engaging—I would say on a monthly basis with each of those leaders—you will not be able to build a close rapport, trust, and confidence.

I would recommend that you set up a monthly cadence call with those four people on the board. It doesn't have to be long; it can be a 10 or 15-minute call. It can be a quick text. It can be an unscheduled quick phone call to say hello and ask their opinion. The key is regularity of monthly touch points to build rapport. If you are distant and not in touch, and they only see you once a quarter, then it's very easy to get out of alignment and for them to not have confidence in your leadership because they don't have insight and they don't have a sense of what is really going on in the company. If they understand how you think and have confidence in how you problem solve and how you set the course for the company, then you will be in good shape.

In the scenario where you are a new CEO for a public company who is recruited from the outside, this to me is the single most vulnerable scenario for a CEO. Here's what often happens: the board determines they need to change the course of the company and that's why they have to seek an outside leader. The internal leaders tend to have a view of incrementally taking the current strategy forward. If the company needs more radical change, they may not have confidence that the internal successors have the radical external perspective needed to take the company in a new direction. For example, let's say that you are Borders Bookstore, and you think that you need to have more online content. And when you look at a traditional bookseller model, you look at the leadership from Borders Bookstore. They don't have online web-centric content curation and outreach direct to consumer on a web go-to market model. So they might, in that case, look to a new CEO outside the company who has deep web expertise. That doesn't mean, however, that the board is actually going to be comfortable with the new agent of change that they have selected to bring in. In fact, what often happens is that they decide they need a new external CEO to help lead change, but then they get nervous and uncomfortable with the change. And the most vulnerable person in a CEO role for a short term is the CEO who's recruited from outside the company. I believe that, in that circumstance, getting alignment around the plan for evolving the company and taking it to a new changed state is a very delicate process that needs a heavy amount of engagement. And that is the circumstance in which you really need very regular board meetings and discussions in between to make sure that there is true buy-in to move forward to a future changed state of the business.

PRIVATE BOARDS

On a private board, the dynamic is slightly different. Again, there will be the same rule of one-third. But since there are no committee chairs, it will likely be your investors, either the senior people from the private equity company or the senior partners from the venture firm. Normally, it's the venture or private equity company that puts the most money in that is the most influential and powerful. Those same senior people will have the say on whether you are supported and continue in your role, or whether they lose confidence. Those senior investors from either venture capital or private equity often have more than one seat. The key people to spend time with are the senior partner and/ or the independent board member whom they nominate to sit in that seat.

Look at your board and figure out who your strongest players are. As in any collection of people, you have one, maybe two, good ones, a couple of neutrals, and a couple of pain in the necks. So you need to engage and co-opt your good ones, and ask them to work with the others and figure out who your go-to people are for different things. And early on, suss that out so that if it's a financing issue, you go to this person; if it's a people leadership team issue, you go here; if it's a strategy question, you go there; if it's a bad behavior question (and there will be those because people have different liquidity horizons, different patience, different maturity levels), you need to have the board member who will help you, the fireman, to deal with the jerk in the boardroom. And you need to co-opt that person early and give them a different status and recognition and engage them to help you. I spend a lot of time between my board meetings with my colleagues getting aligned. Getting engagement and working an issue where there's a disagreement offline is better than hashing out those disagreements in the boardroom. You have to read the tea leaves. This is very important for early stage CEOs. Just as in poker, you have to know when to hold and when to fold, and when to take it off the table and zip it.

KEY TAKE-AWAY

- Determine who on your board are the leaders, gain their support, and engage them on a more regular basis to ensure your longevity as CEO.

CHAPTER 10

CEO SUCCESSION AND SUCCESS

CONTROL YOUR OWN FATE BY TAKING A HARD LOOK IN THE MIRROR AND ASSESSING WHETHER OR NOT YOU HAVE THE SKILLS TO SCALE YOUR COMPANY TO THE NEXT LEVEL.

CEO SUCCESS

How does the board figure this out? And how do you figure it out as the CEO? If this is an early stage company, let's say $0 to $10 million, it is a predictable, known pattern that typically every 18 months, you have to change the entire leadership team. Very, very few CEOs scale all the way and you're better off actually understanding if you're going to scale. Hold

---

TO SUCCESSFULLY SCALE, A CEO MUST:

1. Understand your skills and weaknesses. Delegate.
2. Surround yourself with a strong leadership team and empower them.
3. Communicate, communicate, communicate.

the mirror up and see if you're going to develop as a general manager or not, rather than have it be a really brutal, painful situation where the board tells you that you're just not cutting it and they want to remove you. It would be far better to recognize, as objectively as you can, what the company needs as a general manager and CEO.

For example, during the initial creation of the business plan and the initial funding round, a visionary is necessary, but that doesn't mean that you're the person who can operationalize the vision. Some CEOs can actually execute and operationalize the vision and build a strong team and delegate authority, but most CEOs who are new, green and first-time CEOs have a very hard time with delegating authority and hiring a strong enough executive leadership team. They tend to micromanage and control because that's what has worked in the past. And that's why they were successful: they were able to control things and get the outcomes. But that doesn't scale.

It is far better for you to figure out the role where you can be great, whether it's as the visionary external spokesman, chief strategist, or vice chairman, and graciously move yourself there so that you can continue with the company.

Just as you outgrow the leadership team, so too you outgrow your board, and you need to forward hire along the way. So look at yourself objectively as the CEO and ask yourself, "Am I the right person for zero to $10 million, or zero to $20 million? Am I the right person for when the big inflection happens when we go to $50 million, and then when we break $100 million?" Companies typically stall at $100 million. And then the next big inflection point is when you break $250 million—and then when you get to a billion. So look at your skill set, and try to hire a bunch of leaders who report to you who can help you stay in a role or identify a role where you can continue to contribute. You're better doing it for yourself, because the board is certainly going to figure it out; they will likely figure it out before you recognize it. That's what historically happens. And so it's better to figure it out yourself than have it figured out for you.

YOUR TEAM

Additionally, that same concept for survival as CEO applies to your success as CEO and hiring your leadership team. You outgrow people and their skill sets as the business dynamics and competitive landscape change, as companies keep developing their products and the services they're offering. And it may be, for example, your traditional company that now needs to tech enable, and maybe certain members of your leadership team need to change; maybe you now need a chief digital officer and the traditional legacy chief information officer should report to the chief digital officer. These are the kinds of things that the board will look to you as a leader to recognize as you refresh and hire your team.

The same is true when you think about your board. You should annually charge and request that your governance chair look at effectively taking the same lens to how you're going to grow your business for the one, three and five years ahead. Then map that to the skills of the board members and see if, in fact, the composition of the board is the right composition of perspectives and experiences you need as your company changes. Is it going more global and international? Is it going to grow more inorganically and integrate acquisitions? Is it going to bring on adjacent different products and services that will take the company strategy in a different direction? Is it going to go from being a business-to-business company to a business-to-consumer company?

There are many big changes that strategically your company will take in the one, three and five-year period. This probably should be distilled down for your leadership team, and the board will applaud you for presenting the needs you see for the one, three, and five-year period. It's a less threatening way to actually ask your governance chair to apply that same lens to the profile and skills and abilities of the current board members so that you can see how and when to refresh the board.

Boards should take the lead on CEO performance and assessment for future fit by discussing the type of leadership the company needs. Schedule this review at least annually. The velocity of change is now so fast that many companies hold a multi-day, offsite retreat to shape a forward view of strategy in the competitive landscape. One obvious element of this is to look at current and future leadership, mapping it against your expected future dynamics.

Regarding when and how the board should think about replacing the CEO, start by looking at external data for benchmarks. The average U.S. CEO tenure is now at 9.7 years, according to Forbes. But that assumes a "steady state" company, which is rare in our era of accelerating change. Look at your structural factors. The lifespan of a company according to EquityZen is 11 years before it goes public or is acquired. This helps clarify the question, is the CEO that you have the right CEO for the future?

Assuring a CEO succession plan that aims toward the future can be challenging, especially for smaller companies lacking a deep talent bench. Data show that two-thirds of CEOs developed from within are successful, versus just one-third of external CEOs. But small-cap firms without a strong bench of internal candidates will need the board to extend the annual talent review, discussed above, to think about if/when they may have to look for an outside hire. The current roster may just not be ready for the next stage of the company's growth. Not all CEOs and team members can scale from a $100-500 million company to a far more complex $2 billion one. There will likely need to be an external leadership search. I've found the best way to manage this review at the board level is to make it part of the compensation or governance committee's annual talent assessment.

Speaking of talent assessment, given the stakes your board is dealing with, don't just go with your gut instincts. My boards often use both outside and internal CEO candidate assessments, including psychological screening. These are often handled by executive search firms. Large-cap boards may have a deeper process orientation and formalized CEO succession review. These big companies typically seek an in-depth assessment of the internal candidates to benchmark them against external candidates. Potential leaders should be mapped against where the company needs to take its strategy over the coming three to five years.

For example, a company whose business model and strategy face little significant change, seeking just to execute the core business model through incremental growth and profitability, is likely best served by an internal candidate. Many companies, though, have business models radically impacted by coming change (Sheraton-Hilton lodging model versus Airbnb, or Carey Limousine impacted by Uber). These boards may need to look outside for someone with deeper tech or innovation skills or fresh business model expertise to help the firm cross the competitive chasm.

The board's leadership planning shouldn't focus just on individual talents but also on how the role itself is structured. In the U.S., combining the jobs of chief executive and board chair has long been the de facto model. There has been some erosion in this leadership norm though. Currently, just half of S&P 500 companies split the two roles, compared with three-quarters of British FTSE 100 companies (the FTSE has a "comply or explain" policy on dividing the jobs). In America, if the CEO is not ultimately named board chair, it's viewed negatively. For example, in the case of a successful, iconic CEO, such as Nike's Mark Parker, it would be seen as demeaning not to be awarded the chairman role.

In CEO succession, the point when a CEO retires and a new CEO arrives is a convenient window for splitting the CEO and chair roles. Naming a retired CEO to become chairman of the board is often a sticky situation though. The new CEO often feels second-guessed by the former chief. The chairman/former CEO may have a very hard time letting go of operational responsibilities, and your board may have inadvertently set up a dynamic with high risk and many negatives. I would advise boards to think long and hard before they put a retired CEO into the chairman role.

When boards agree to this structure, I fear they're often not facing the really hard decisions. It's always awkward and difficult for a board to transition a founder. The founder feels ownership for his or her company and has

THIS DYNAMIC GROWS EVEN MORE COMPLICATED WHEN A RETIRING CEO IS ALSO THE COMPANY FOUNDER. A FOUNDER WHO RETIRES AS CEO TO TAKE ON AN EMERITUS BOARD CHAIR SLOT IS A FORMULA FOR VERY HIGH RISK. THERE ARE VERY FEW EXAMPLES WHERE THIS HAS WORKED SUCCESSFULLY—AND MANY MORE WHERE IT HAS HURT THE PERFORMANCE OF THE COMPANY AND HAS SIGNIFICANTLY DISTRACTED THE NEW CEO.

many deep relationships. It is extraordinarily difficult for a founder who is emeritus chairman to stick to the boardroom parameters, not overstepping and inserting him/herself into operations.

In weighing a founder emeritus chairmanship, boards must ask themselves if they truly are the 1 in 100 (or even 1 in 1,000 case) that will work. Consider carefully the risks of destabilizing the new CEO for the shareholders. A better approach is for the board to shape a special advisor role for the founder, assigning special, targeted projects. One example might be to define a one-year role to specifically assist in some predefined areas in the transition to the new CEO.

KEY TAKE-AWAY

- CEO succession should be looked at every year by the board.
- Internal pipelines should be reviewed to ensure a successor bench is being built.

BOARD LEARNINGS: A COLLECTION OF CASE STUDIES AND PUBLISHED ARTICLES

INTRODUCTION

Throughout my 20-plus years of board service, I have had the benefit of serving on some really stellar boards where the directors truly partner to mentor and contribute actively with the CEO and his leadership team. While still one of oversight, the role of the board has changed to a much more engaged and active accelerant for the company and its strategic initiatives.

The articles below are some of my most recent writings on the velocity of change that companies are experiencing through technology and the impact of digitization, activists, ESG, and scandals in the boardroom. I hope they are helpful as you start your journey to becoming an active and engaged board member.

INSIDE THE BOARDROOM: SCANDAL SPECIALISTS

By Betsy Atkins

Allegations of misconduct, fraud and corruption are everywhere lately, with nearly every news cycle surfacing a tale that seems to bear investigation. Just last month, charges of sexual misconduct by CBS CEO Les Moonves surfaced, coming shortly on the heels of the news that Papa John's besieged founder and chairman, John Schnatter, had been unseated by his latest alleged verbal transgression.

Massive data breaches, accounting fraud, corruption, harassment—whatever the scandal du jour—internally, the task of sussing out just what happened and where any fault may lie falls to the board. It's a gargantuan responsibility—one made more difficult by the speed with which crisis-fueled events unfold and the level of scrutiny they spawn.

A well-handled internal investigation can go a long way toward mitigating the potential fallout of alleged wrongdoing, helping to restore a company's reputation and reduce the risk of legal exposure and material impact. Here's a three-step approach to navigating that process.

SHOULD YOU INVESTIGATE?

From a whistle-blower report of wrongdoing to an auditor bringing a serious lapse to your attention, any number of red flags might suggest that an investigation could be warranted. It's your job to decide if this issue requires the board to step in, rather than a response from the executive team.

Ask yourselves, "Is the company's ability to conduct an independent investigation impaired?" Assurances from the C-suite alone should not suffice. CEO Ken Lay conducted an investigation at Enron and reported that nothing was amiss. We know how well that worked out.

In certain circumstances, the potential for liability comes into play. For example, when a shareholder derivative suit is underway, a special committee investigation may be warranted to address the charges in the suit and help immunize the company against liability. Both the company and the board have a legal obligation to actively monitor and ensure legal compliance and internal controls.

WHO SHOULD INVESTIGATE?

If the board opts to investigate, an independent committee of the board should be formed. That committee should be chartered by the board as a whole with a specific mandate, powers and timeline.

While you can empower your current audit or governance committee, a dedicated subcommittee of the board has advantages and lets you shape membership to address the unique problem at hand and to write its own charter for investigation. In this charter, you should:

- Spell out the matters to be investigated and make clear the committee's powers.
- Name the members of the committee.
- Set a scope and timeline.

- Define the outcome sought. Is the committee charged solely with investigating or will it also be recommending action to the full board or taking that action itself?

Understand that throughout this process, you will be second-guessed by management, the media, and stakeholders. Thorough ground work, rigorous planning, and strict protocols will help insulate the investigation from these outside pressures.

HOW SHOULD THE INVESTIGATION BE CONDUCTED?

This is no process for amateurs. The committee should hire independent, nonaffiliated corporate counsel to structure the investigation for maximum legal protection. Counsel or other investigatory professionals from outside the firm should be brought in and charged by the committee to do the actual digging. Counsel can suggest and advise on who within or outside the company may need to be "quarantined" from the investigation, or even from their current functions.

The more serious an allegation and the higher up in the organization culpability may extend, the more likely an outside law firm should carry out the investigation.

Work with counsel to keep as much of the investigation and findings legally privileged. The board should keep its hands out of the actual investigating.

After counsel and independent external resources (accountants, professional investigators, etc.) look into the matter, they should report back to the committee. Process is important here—the sleuthing investigators should not report to or share information with management. In some cases, even a formal written report is unwise. Instead, investigating counsel could present its findings to the committee in an oral report. The committee will then report to the full board, which may question the committee and counsel at a full board meeting. The board should ask probing questions of those who make the report.

Assuming the investigation turns up some misconduct, the board will face tough questions: Should a formal report be written? When and how should the CEO be briefed on the findings? Should the company make voluntary disclosures to the government or regulators in hope of leniency? How much should be disclosed, and when? Advisers can help guide you through these decisions.

Ultimately, circumstances and context will factor into the investigation process. However, in today's scandal-strewn corporate environment, all directors need an understanding of the best practices for conducting investigations.

Adapted from Corporate Board Member Magazine September 24, 2018.

KEY TAKE-AWAY

When allegations against a company are made, the board must determine if an internal investigation is needed and if a special committee should be formed, who will lead it, what their mandate will be, and what kind of recommendations they can make.

ENVIRONMENT, SOCIAL & GOVERNANCE

By Betsy Atkins

(I wrote the following article to present the argument for proactively addressing ESG issues through formal corporate governance policies.)

Environmental, social and governance (ESG) issues should be a top concern of corporate management and boards. There was a time when a public stance on ESG issues was a public relations tactic. However, in today's rapidly changing business climate, attention to ESG issues is becoming critical to long-term competitive success.

Major institutional investors recognize this and are making it clear that they expect the companies they hold to take a proactive approach to ESG policies and messaging. In his annual letter to CEOs, BlackRock's CEO Larry Fink wrote that "a company's ability to manage environmental, social, and governance matters demonstrate the leadership and good governance that is so essential to sustainable growth, which is why we are increasingly integrating these issues into our investment process." During the 2017 proxy season, State Street Global Advisors (SSGA) put this ethos into action by voting against the re-election of directors at 400 companies that SSGA said failed to make any significant effort to appoint women to their all-male boards.

The advantages of proactively tackling ESG issues go beyond appeasing institutional shareholders and creating a good public relations story. A robust ESG program can open up access to large pools of capital, build a stronger corporate brand, and promote sustainable long-term growth benefitting companies and investors. Here's how:

1. STRONG ESG PROGRAMS CAN INCREASE STOCK LIQUIDITY.

Individual and institutional investors alike are investing massive pools of capital in corporations that proactively govern and operate in an ethical and sustainable manner. Sustainable and impact investing is actively growing at double-digit rates. In fact, according to the US SIF Foundation, total U.S.-domiciled investments using sustainable, responsible and impact (SRI) strategies reached $8.72 trillion, an increase of 33 percent from 2014 and a 14-fold increase since 1995. That represents about 1 of every 6 dollars under management.

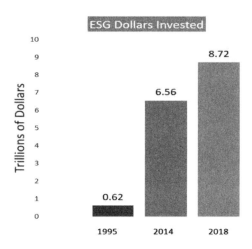

Investment research and consulting firms, such as Sustainanalytics and MSCI, have developed indices that measure and rank companies based upon ESG criteria relative to their industry peers. The investment funds and ETFs that benchmark these indices are raising trillions of dollars to be deployed toward companies that execute sound ESG policies; these are long-term oriented shareholders that can potentially fuel demand for your stock. Many investment firms are also incorporating ESG evaluations in their portfolio risk assessment, which is a telling indicator that capital will continue to flow toward companies with strong ESG programs and practices.

2. ESG INITIATIVES CAN UNLOCK COMPETITIVE VALUE.

Companies that recognize the importance of adapting to changing socio-economic and environmental conditions are better able to identify strategic opportunities and meet competitive challenges. Proactive and integrated ESG policies can widen a company's competitive moat relative to other industry players.

Starbucks (Nasdaq: SBUX) learned this as they were trying to expand their market share in China. For years after entering that market, Starbucks struggled to gain momentum on expansion. They stumbled upon the answer when they offered healthcare to their employees' parents. Once they did that, sales growth skyrocketed and now Starbucks has 2,000 stores in one of the fastest growing markets on the globe.

Executives who take steps to improve labor conditions, enhance the diversity of their teams, give back to their communities, and take a stand on sustainable environmental policies also strengthen the company's brand. As millennials in particular become employees, consumers, and investors, they take note of good corporate actors and reward them with loyalty.

3. A PROACTIVE STANCE ON ESG ISSUES CAN KEEP ACTIVISTS AT BAY.

Activists have used governance weaknesses as a tool in proxy contests and campaigns against companies for years, but increasingly they are targeting management teams and boards that fail to take a proactive stance on potential environmental or social issues.

Companies that proactively address ESG issues can set the bar for the entire industry and at the same time help immunize themselves against activist intervention. Wynn Resorts (NASDAQ: WYNN) recently embraced their commitment to gender diversity by increasing the number of women on their board from one to four. With a board that is 36 percent female, Wynn is now in the top 40 S&P 500 companies in terms of female board representation. If your company does become the target of an ESG-focused activist, don't despair. Activist investment firms and hedge funds are establishing their own ESG funds, such as ValueAct Capital and Jana Partners. Many of these investors are interested in collaborating with companies to develop ESG policies that unlock the long-term value we mentioned above. For example, Jeff Ubben, CEO of ValueAct Capital, recently joined the board of energy company AES Corporation to help continue the company's transition to clean and renewable energy sources (following divestiture of its coal assets).

4. ESG INVESTORS ARE "STICKIER."

ESG investors are values-based investors who are more interested in what happens during the next decade than the next quarter; they understand that change takes time. Investors incorporating ESG into their mandate often work alongside a company to strengthen it, as they are more interested in building long-term value over a multi-year period than in flipping the stock in the near term for a "sugar high."

5. COMPANIES THAT ESPOUSE STRONG ESG VALUES TEND TO ATTRACT AND RETAIN THE BEST TALENT.

Millennials care deeply that the companies they work for (and the businesses they support) embrace values that are aligned with their own, and environmental and social responsibility are very important to them. Employees who are passionate about the organization, who are loyal, and who feel valued drive an intangible goodwill that strengthens the brand of the company and improves the overall productivity of the workforce.

BEST PRACTICES

To realize the full benefit of a proactive stance on ESG issues, it's important to adhere to some best practices for benchmarking and strengthening the company's ESG program:

Identify the appropriate ESG criteria for your industry and your company.

When developing an ESG policy framework, companies should not try to be all things to all people. Rather, identify three to five measurable ESG criteria that are material to your businesses and your constituencies, and are aligned with your corporate strategies.

For example, an oil and gas company that is fracking should measure water and waste management and impacts on scarce natural resources. If your business is centered around service personnel as Starbucks is, social training on anti-harassment and racial sensitivity will make consumers feel welcome and will strengthen the corporate brand. Wynn Resorts, as a business that delivers premium services to clientele, focuses on employment initiatives to ensure they attract and retain the best workforce: workplace safety and sensitivity, gender equality, a Women's Leadership Forum, and diversity and inclusion. Wynn Resorts also addresses the environmental impacts of their large hotel properties. They recycle 95 percent of the water they use, and many properties are LEED certified. Wynn Las Vegas just announced a multi-use development, Paradise Park, powered by 100 percent renewable energy sourced from a 160-acre solar energy facility, making it one of the most environmentally conscious planned developments in Las Vegas.

An effective way to benchmark your company's ESG framework relative to your peers is to research industry rankings within a major sustainability ranking index. There are a number of nonprofit global advocacy organizations that identify and rank corporate ESG programs:

1. Global Reporting Initiative (GRI)
2. Sustainability Accounting Standards Board (SASB)
3. Global Initiative for Sustainability Rankings (GISR)

These organizations, as well as ESG advisory companies such as Sustainanalytics and MSCI, analyze a broad range of criteria for each industry, only some of which include climate change impacts, natural resource scarcity, supply chain management, labor practices, political contributions, board composition, and workplace diversity and inclusion. The influence of proxy advisory firms like ISS and Glass Lewis over institutional investors has grown in recent years, so reviewing the governance scores they apply to your company can be another useful benchmark.

Pursue inclusion within relevant ESG indices.

As mentioned above, inclusion in ESG index funds and/or ETFs can boost demand for and liquidity in your company's stock. Once your company has identified the elements of its ESG framework, have your general counsel contact three or four ESG funds or ETFs to research their criteria for inclusion (and exclusion). From there, identify which of these indices map most closely to your corporate strategy and to the priorities of the shareholder base that you believe represent your best long-term holders.

Most ESG pools of capital apply their own unique set of inclusion and/or exclusion criteria to determine which companies to include. For example, to qualify for inclusion in the FTSE4Good Index Series, companies must be working toward environmental sustainability, supporting universal human rights, ensuring good supply-chain labor standards, countering bribery, and mitigating and adapting to climate change. Companies that have been identified as having business interests in tobacco, nuclear weapons systems, or firearms, however, are excluded from that series.

TELL YOUR STORY AND STAY TRUE TO IT.

Once your company has determined the appropriate criteria for its ESG framework, the next steps are to establish metrics, measure them on a regular basis, and share progress publicly; otherwise, you will be accused of "greenwashing." Companies that are guilty of greenwashing spin a PR narrative of high standards for environmental protections and human rights but don't walk the talk. Greenwashing is going to become harder to get away with as the SEC increasingly calls for companies to file corporate social responsibility and sustainability reports.

Investors have a number of criteria they use to determine whether a company is greenwashing or truly integrating ESG policies in their business practices. Companies that are truly committed to executing their ESG policies make them a senior management priority of the CEO and general counsel, and tie compensation to ESG metrics. They voluntarily report ESG goals, and progress toward meeting them, to all stakeholders via the annual CEO letter, annual reports, internal corporate communications, and/or annual sustainability reports on the corporate website.

Adapted from NASDAQ Listing Center, June 5, 2018.

KEY TAKE-AWAY

Your company's presentation of their Environmental, Social and Governance profile is becoming critical to gaining access to significant pools of capital as well as long-term competitive success.

ENVIRONMENTAL, SOCIAL & GOVERNANCE– VOLVO CARS USE CASE

By Betsy Atkins

As a follow-up to how companies may embrace Environmental, Social and Governance issues, I use Volvo Cars where I am a board member as an example and use case.

Volvo has a significant, fulsome Sustainability Program with CEO top-down support. Volvo solidified its commitment to sustainability in 2017 by adding sustainability to the People and Compensation Committee with sustainability being directly addressed by the committee twice a year in addition to the board's oversight. Our general counsel owns and leads our program.

Some of the highlights of Volvo's programs are the following:

- Volvo announced their electrification program in 2017, stating that it was going all electric by 2019. Volvo will accomplish this by adding the option of electric motors to every model.

- They have further enhanced their electrification plans with an announcement that they aim for 50 percent of sales to be fully electric by 2025. That's a significantly more aggressive goal than adding electric options to all models.
- Volvo has committed to being climate neutral in manufacturing by 2025.
- All plastics in cars will be recycled but tested for strength and safety, including carpets from recycled materials.
- Use of Sustainalytics to measure specific targets on reduction of CO_2.
- Volvo will use only responsible leather (as determined by traceability, respecting animal welfare) as well as offering leather-free options.
- Commitment to LEED certified gold standard: new buildings will comply with LEED standards and old buildings will be refurbished seeking LEED compliance. (LEED, which stands for Leadership in Energy and Environmental Design, is a global certification program focused primarily on new commercial building projects. Different levels of certification are based upon a points system.)
- Measuring overall company renewable energy use (in Sweden, 100 percent).
- Volvo is the top 3 auto company in the world in health and safety, including contractors.
- Moving from a linear economy: "take, make, dispose" to regenerative circular economy based on recycle and reuse, making the most out of finite resources. This includes the subscription business model, which is circular where Volvo retains ownership of the assets in the car subscription.
- Volvo responsibly sources for cobalt batteries (no conflict minerals from the Congo and no child labor).
- Volvo has been reporting on sustainability since 2003.

As part of their annual report, Volvo Cars presents a sustainability score-card[1] showing improvements and enhancements over the last five years so that investors and consumers can clearly see their commitment to Environmental, Social, and Governance issues. Volvo's sustainability scorecard has four distinct dimensions: economic, environmental, people, and social.

Their key economic indicator is the number of units sold, which has improved since 2013 from 427,840 units to 571,577. This is key in understanding the remaining dimensions. Increasing output and sales would normally increase use of energy or water in manufacturing, so it's important to have a set point of what is being measured.

Volvo has several environmental dimensions, including energy use (which has decreased even with increased production and sales). Energy use per manufactured vehicle has decreased as well from 1.3 megawatt-hour/vehicle in 2013 to 1.1 in 2017. In addition to energy use, emissions, waste, water and materials usage are all reported with significant reductions over the five-year reporting period.

Volvo's commitment to the people dimension is clear as they have made significant strides in increasing the number of women in leading positions from 22.9 percent in 2013 to 28 percent in 2017. Reductions in numbers of injuries, accidents, and sick leave are also dramatic over the five-year period. Lost Time Case Rate, the standard measure by which companies measure the cost of sick leave, has declined from .62 in 2013 to .19 in 2017.

Finally, Volvo has a social dimension that indicates the percentage of product categories for which health and safety impacts are assessed for improvement. Volvo assesses 100 percent of its product categories. They do not selectively pick and choose which categories would be most beneficial for their reporting (greenwashing).

Sustainability at Volvo Cars is governed by the sustainability board, which is a decision-making body responsible for directing and monitoring

---

1   "Sustainability," Electrification | Volvo Car Group, 2017, group.volvocars.com/sustainability.

Volvo's sustainability program. The sustainability board consists of the president and CEO as well as a number of executive management team members. The board is chaired by the senior vice president and general counsel, group legal and corporate governance.

Beyond annual reporting, Volvo keeps its commitment to sustainability in the forefront of daily operations with the sustainability working group, which consists of the operational leads and meets fortnightly to discuss emerging opportunities and challenges, as well as to share best practice and ongoing initiatives. The working group is chaired by the director of sustainability and reports to the sustainability board.

Volvo has been reporting on the environmental, health and safety aspects of its products and production since it signed the UN Global Compact in 2000. In 2003, the company produced its first sustainability report in line with the international reporting guidelines from the Global Reporting Initiative (GRI). In 2018 the sustainability portion of the annual report will be externally verified by a third party.

By embracing ESG, companies will find, as Volvo has found, that a sustainable approach not only brings environmental and social benefits, but it also enhances the appeal of a company's products, enhances profitability, engages employees, and helps attract the best talent.

Adapted from Forbes, December 4, 2018.

KEY TAKE-AWAY

Environment, social and governance programs should be created and presented in a way that shows consistent improvements across time, should outline a selection of parameters that make sense for your company, and should include outside verification by a third party.

INSIDE THE BOARDROOM WITH BETSY ATKINS

"There's often no better source of information than a person who has stood in your shoes. So in that spirit, we've asked boardroom insider Betsy Atkins to offer advice on concerns submitted by readers. This quarter, she addresses issues related to ESG proxy proposals, D&O insurance, ERM, and on-boarding new directors."

Dear Betsy,

We seem to be hearing a lot about proxy proposals related to environmental and social concerns. Which of these types of proxy items do I as a board member need to be ready for?

There is a significant increase in environmental, social and governance (ESG) proxy items. First, there's a high probability that companies are going to need to report on sustainability efforts, as environmental groups are pushing hard for that. The UK Corporate Governance Code already encompasses sustainability in its corporate social responsibility (CSR) score, much in the same way ISS sets standards for corporate governance in the United States. Moreover, the standard-setters, such as CSR RepTrak system, are now measuring a company's ability to deliver on stakeholder expectations across three dimensions of CSR: (1) citizenship (support of good causes, positive societal influence, and environmental responsibility); (2) governance (openness and transparency, ethical behavior, and fair business practices); and (3) workplace (fair employee rewards, employee well-being, and equal opportunities). Therefore, it's very likely that one of the next priority items to appear on many proxies will be proposals around this sustainability theme, so boards would be well advised to start looking into preparing a sustainability report on an annual basis. These reports are somewhat complicated because there are a variety of metrics and standards to select from. Because shareholders are increasingly valuing sustainability and some stakeholders will loudly pursue it, it is advisable to start doing some early homework here.

Dear Betsy,
Do you feel it's acceptable to have the in-house GC handle our board's director and officer (D&O) insurance review, or should we use an outside specialist?

I strongly recommend using an outside legal expert who focuses exclusively on director and officer insurance. One really valuable aspect of this is having an outside law firm look at the D&O insurance language to make sure there are no exclusions buried in the policy. Keep in mind, you generally only need your D&O policy when something seriously bad is happening, and that's the wrong time to find out if the language has been written by the insurance provider in a way that excludes you from the coverage you thought you had. Additionally, it is very valuable to have your outside expert look at specific topics where you as a director are especially vulnerable, such as Foreign Corrupt Practices Act/ anti-bribery and cyber insurance coverage. It is also very wise to have a review of your indemnification to make sure it is up to the most recent Delaware standards and is as broad as possible to protect you. Having a dedicated outside professional who knows the ins and outs of these technical areas is a good investment for the board.

Dear Betsy,

Do you have any advice on how to create a risk matrix for setting boardroom agenda priorities? Enterprise risk management (ERM) is something we hear a lot about, but our board struggles with how to get our arms around it.

Creating a matrix of the company's biggest risks and getting alignment from management and the board on the top risks facing the company is a very healthy practice. Your question is an excellent one, since it takes ERM from an audit committee risk mitigation exercise to a front-and-center focus to pinpoint the biggest challenges the corporation faces on an annual basis. In order to identify the most crucial product, competitive market, and financial risks, the board must collaborate as a team to establish which business issues should be covered as specific agenda items during the major quarterly meetings. The outcome of the discussion would be a series of agenda topics that require management to go deep on the major risks and detail its plan to address each risk and mitigate it. Going through such an exercise allows directors to delve into overall strategic risk so that the board can look at it carefully on behalf of shareholders.

Dear Betsy,

The best way to on-board new directors is something our board has grappled with for years in terms of figuring out how to bring new directors up to speed and get them ready for all that board service throws at them. Some of our directors say that a mentoring period can be a useful practice, but that seems like such a big commitment. Do you have any experience with this, or can you offer advice from your board experiences about successful on-boarding strategies?

Successful new-director on-boarding should set two-way engagement expectations. The board, typically with support from the GC and corporate secretary, should provide an orientation for new directors, who come in early, perhaps a half or full day in advance of their first board meeting. Ideally, a series of one-on-one meetings with a subset of the CEO's direct reports will help a new director get a current frame of reference on the company as part of his or her on-boarding. Spending time with the CFO, business unit presidents, or key functional leaders, such as the head of product or sales, is also especially valuable. If the company is a manufacturer, having the chance to tour the factory with the vice president of manufacturing is beneficial; likewise, if the company is a retailer, organizing field trips to visit stores is especially valuable. For example, when I joined the Volvo board, I spent several hours touring the safety/crash labs, which offered insights I could not have gained otherwise.

Additionally, having a package of financial and industry analyst reports, along with one or two previous board packages, provides good context for new board members. As far as mentoring, I would recommend new directors try to spend some one-on-one time with their colleagues to get the "institutional memory" of current board members on the most important priorities, opportunities and risks the company has dealt with and is likely to face going forward. And while audit committee service will likely not be something a new director is thrown into, some companies feel it is especially valuable for new directors to listen in or join the audit committee, as the issues on its agenda often provide a very holistic view of the corporation and current risks.

Adapted from Corporate Board Member, Q2 2017.

KEY TAKE-AWAY

As a board member, you should keep current on topics like: ESG, D&O review, enterprise risk management, and on-boarding new directors.

UNFRIENDLY SKIES FOR PETS?

By Betsy Atkins

With the death of a dog in flight, it may be time for the United Airlines board to revisit their brand's values and vision, and the importance of living up to them.

United's customer service curse struck again last week with the death of a passenger's French bulldog, after the flight crew forced the pooch to be placed in an overhead bin on a Houston to New York flight. And just a day afterward, the airline goofed again, accidentally shipping a Kansas City-bound family's German shepherd to Japan.

According to U.S. Department of Transportation figures, United's death and injury rate for animals in transport is more than double that of all other U.S. airlines. When 62 percent of American's own a pet, the result is a body blow to public confidence in United.

Of course, United has even bigger problems with the way it treats people. We all saw the gruesome cellphone footage from last year of a passenger being dragged off an overbooked flight. Such mis-bookings, seat mix-ups, threats, and even assaults to passengers fill any news search on "United Airlines."

No doubt a mega-enterprise like United has plenty of people and systems to blame for abusing their consumers and damaging their own brand. But such a widespread failure cannot be separated from United's overall corporate culture.

This meltdown starts at the very top—the United Airlines board of directors has the opportunity to ask management to come up with a plan to change the culture to being more passenger-centric.

United is one more dismal example of corporate culture not putting the customer first. Their net promoter score is one of the lowest in the industries, and their Glassdoor employee score shows a serious lack of morale (as an example of the latter, last week United management tried limiting worker bonuses to a "lottery" system, which stirred employee outrage).

All of this translates into a terrible experience both for passengers and the workers who interact with them.

For a public corporation, public image is a fiduciary concern. If United is viewed as the airline that treats people like animals (and animals as expendable), the result is loss of consumer loyalty, which drives down ridership and inevitably hurts the stock price.

The United board members must take this breakdown seriously and mandate a cultural reboot.

Company culture, starting with the tone at the top, is always the ultimate driver of company performance, no matter the business model. As Peter Drucker wrote, culture eats strategy for breakfast.

The lack of empathy and concern for their customers and passengers is hurting the shareholders, and the United board has the opportunity to make serious changes in the culture.

The board first needs to insist on retraining for all of their employees to become more customer-centric. And while they're at it, directors can hold management's feet to the fire for regaining the trust of those customers. In any consumer business, both customers and employees are ultimately stakeholders, with the power to make or break the company.

The board should also set specific numerical metrics to measure and improve the company culture. The compensation committee can tie significant portions of the leadership team's pay to these metrics. For example, the net promoter score for customer satisfaction, measurement of customer complaints, and retraining of all customer-facing touch points are among cultural measures that can be objectively scored.

Some of these reforms will be a challenge, since management will have to negotiate with their unions, who doubtless have little goodwill at the moment. But this cultural refit needs to be done. There must be a system to rapidly replace consistently poor-performing employees who shred consumer loyalty.

The historic company slogan of "fly the friendly skies of United" is now a laughing stock. The airline's culture demands a total reboot, with metrics tied to performance bonuses so that service delights passengers rather than horrifies them.

A board-driven rediscovery of the "friendly skies" culture can rebuild both a stronger airline and a stronger-performing stock for shareholders.

Adapted from The Directors & Boards, March 22, 2018.

KEY TAKE-AWAY

Ensuring that corporate culture and public image are customer-centric should be a board concern. Review your company's corporate culture before it turns into a PR disaster.

ACTIVISM'S NEW PARADIGM

By Gregory Taxin and Betsy Atkins

Editor's note: Gregory Taxin is Managing Director at Spotlight Advisors and Betsy Atkins is an American business executive and entrepreneur. This article is based on a publication that originally appeared in *Corporate Board Member* magazine. Related research from the Program on Corporate Governance includes "The Long-Term Effects of Hedge Fund Activism" by Lucian Bebchuk, Alon Brav, and Wei Jiang; "The Myth that Insulating Boards Serves Long-Term Value" by Lucian Bebchuk; and "Who Bleeds When the Wolves Bite? A Flesh-and-Blood Perspective on Hedge Fund Activism and Our Strange Corporate Governance System" by Leo E. Strine, Jr.—all cited at the end of this article.

Shareholder activism in the US has increased greatly over the past decade, measured not only in scope and the pools of capital dedicated to it but also in sophistication and in the range of tactics employed. There is currently more than $120 billion in dedicated activist funds at work, and these funds launched nearly 300 activist campaigns globally in 2016. Another 400 campaigns were launched by "occasional" activists. Indeed, a fair number of companies should expect a knock at their door soon—21 percent of the S&P 500 were approached publicly by an activist in 2016 according to FactSet (and many others received quiet, private overtures). Such activism will likely grow more prevalent, as it has proven to generate alpha (i.e., uncorrelated returns) for these funds' investors.

Activists and activism draw sharp emotional responses: some cheer activists as appropriate scolds of lazy and underperforming boards; others paint activists as locusts focused solely on short-term strategies. Activism is a natural outgrowth of our market's structure and can be a force for good. All capital markets need a mechanism to "police" strategy selection and board performance in those rare instances when the corporate governance system does not work.

For the most part, our system of corporate governance does work and boards self-correct to put companies on the optimal strategic path. But the board mechanism is not perfect: Not all boards are as independent as they ought to be and directors also have some interests, such as director fees and job continuity, that differ from shareholders.

For these reasons and others, activists can and do play an important role as last-resort overseers of the shareholders' interests, but as in every human endeavor, some perform better than others.

Activist techniques were once used only by specialist funds. Now, traditional, long-term investors are adopting (and adapting) activist techniques, increasing the volume of shareholder engagements. They've seen that engagement at companies with suboptimal strategies or underperforming management teams can help generate alpha. It can also help justify the larger fees charged by active managers. At the same time, some specialized activist funds are taking a longer-term view of performance.

All of these factors are driving a new wave of shareholder activism, with campaigns often reaching outside traditional targets. Companies of all sizes and types can have "opinionated" stockholders.

Today, in fact, even good stock performance does not immunize a company. Take the recent example of restaurant chain Buffalo Wild Wings. Over the 14 years since the company went public in 2003, the stock compounded shareholders' money by 24 percent per year, dramatically outperforming its casual dining peers. On operating metrics, the business also outperformed nearly all of its peers. In the three years before this spring's proxy battle, the stock was up 18 percent in a difficult sector, where many of its peers had gone belly up. Yet, even strong performance like this did not protect Buffalo Wild Wings from Marcato Capital's advances and demands.

FUNDAMENTAL DRIVERS

What are the drivers of activist campaigns? Activists are, first and foremost, investors. They seek great returns and they propose changes that they believe will drive better future performance than the market expects. In this way, the driver of activist activity is really perceived suboptimal plans, not suboptimal past performance. The tactical focus is often on strategy, operations, the balance sheet, business configuration, the board, and M&A.

Activists are often extremely knowledgeable about the company, very invested in future outcomes, and equipped with analytical tools that can outstrip even a well-meaning board.

Ultimately, an activist must be able to answer the question, why hasn't the board adopted the proposed changes? And so, activists necessarily focus on perceived deficiencies in board composition or on a claim that the board is "stale." Naturally, then, boards with longer average director tenure are significantly more vulnerable to campaigns. If there is a deficiency in strategy or business configuration and the board is seen as "stale," then the activist can claim that the staleness has led to the suboptimal choices.

Activist campaigns are remarkably successful, in part because activists get to pick their targets. In well over half of the campaigns, significant changes are driven by the activist. CEO tenures are shorter and, according to some academics, stock performance is better, once an activist appears.

A 2017 survey by FTI Consulting finds that settlements have become more prevalent and have come quicker than in the past. Nevertheless, more fights in absolute numbers went to a final vote in 2016 than at any time since 2010.

The increased number of companies facing activist campaigns has been driven by nontraditional activists. Mainstream, long-only institutional investors and first-time or "occasional" activists account for nearly all the increased volume in activism. Recent examples include campaigns by Neuberger Berman, T. Rowe Price, and PAR Capital Management, all three of which had been regarded as traditional investors that "vote with their feet" rather than vocally.

Activism is becoming a tactic deployed by all types of investors rather than a "strategy" that defines a fund. Along with its broader adoption, the practice of activism has professionalized, with a bevy of advisors that help both investors and companies to engage in these campaigns.

Given the willingness of more investors to use activist tactics, every public company may have activists in its shareholder base. The lurking activist may not have a familiar activist fund name: it may be your long-tenured shareholder who wants to be heard. Some activists are hidden in plain sight.

PLANNING STRATEGICALLY

For public company board members, these changes bring a new reality of engaged investors, with heightened reputational stakes for directors. Noisy, public campaigns challenge the judgment and composition of the board. And proxy fights are more distracting and expensive than is often imagined. In fact, it's hard to overstate the all-consuming nature of such battles. Having been involved in more than fifty activist campaigns, we can tell you definitively that once embroiled in a proxy fight, the CEO, CFO, and board members will be forced to spend substantial time dealing with tough, daily decisions, and the costs often run between $4 million and $6 million for a full campaign at a mid-cap company. These costs have been escalating as campaigns go on longer and often involve many advisors: some protracted fights will cost a company well over $20 million. Obviously, some battles are worth fighting, but remember the odds: Companies very often lose—and will get stuck with the bill and distraction anyway.

The best defense is to make smart governance moves in times of peace. Since long-tenured boards have proven to be an easy wedge for activists, boards must proactively consider their refreshment, casting a critical eye on the mix of tenures and expertise. Think about setting a target "average tenure" for the board as a governance policy. It's rare to find a well-composed, self-refreshing board come under successful attack from an activist.

Structural and strategic moves also help avoid activist campaigns before they begin. The board and management should lead an active, objective review and analysis of popular activist hot-button issues (e.g., capital allocation, capital structure, strategy, operational plans, executive compensation, business configuration, personnel, etc.). One good option is to bring in a third party to help the board "think like an activist" to provide fresh input and objective thinking and identify vulnerabilities (which can be opportunities for improvement) ahead of time.

RESPONSE TACTICS THAT WORK

Creative thinking on investor relations is also crucial. Consider "radical transparency" with investors about the roads taken and the roads not taken. Why did your company take a different path than peer companies? Directors must be prepared to provide rationales about choices made and differences in operating models, strategies, or performance.

Even with the above tactics, a surprise activist campaign involving your company is always possible. How do you respond? As a first step, the board should be immediately informed, should ensure there is a response team, and should designate a representative to liaise with the team.

Most companies turn to their corporate counsel first. And while counsel is critical in these situations, remember that an opinionated investor is not primarily a legal problem. Advisors can be helpful, but too many can be unwieldy.

It is critical to know where your other shareholders stand on the points raised by the activist. But be cautious in assuming that management knows the true feelings of your shareholder base. Investors don't always tell their true feelings to management.

The management team should actively engage with would-be activists to understand their thesis and points of view. At first, activists almost always seem friendly and express a desire to engage "constructively." Be wary. At the same time, always remember that being gracious pays off.

The company must contemplate its approach and words carefully, depending on the activist. Your board can prove a great asset in this engagement. Ensure that one or more directors are designated to speak to investors, should the need arise. (We recognize that many corporate advisers prefer to hide the board from investors. This approach, though common, has serious risks in our experience. Directors are shareholders' representatives and should be willing to meet with those whom they represent.) Whoever speaks for the company should know that there may be a tricky dance required to be both open and compliant with disclosure rules. This is especially true because activists often suggest things that are actively being considered or are under way, which makes for difficult conversations if the company's activities are not already public.

SIX QUESTIONS YOU SHOULD ADDRESS BEFORE AN ACTIVIST DOES

Activists today are professionals who know your company inside and out—sometimes better than management. Here are six questions the board and management should answer internally before they find themselves on the defensive with an activist:

1. How does the company's performance compare with its peers? How do valuation metrics compare, as well as executive compensation programs?

2. What does the buy side think of your strategy and operational prowess (not what you'd like to hope they think)?

3. What does the competition say, and what do its leaders think are your company's strengths and weaknesses?

4. How are your incumbent directors and management vulnerable?

5. What guidance has the management team provided that proved too optimistic?

6. What are the impediments to board self-evaluation and refreshment?

In meeting with the activist, avoid defensiveness and a closed mind. Consider elements from an activist's agenda that you can adopt, leaving him or her with fewer complaints and suggestions.

Activist investors often have reasonable ideas worth considering, so be open to contemplating those ideas objectively.

The hardest "suggestions" usually are requests for changes to the board. As noted earlier, preemptive board refreshment is often the best medicine. Post-activist unilateral appointment of new directors is certainly not as good as preemptive board refreshment, but it's still better in many cases than remaining static with a board slate that is difficult to defend. Consider the options of agreeing to a third-party board candidate approved by both sides, setting a plan of refreshment, or appointing an alternative stockholder representative.

If you find yourself embroiled in a full, public proxy battle, early moves and press releases will set the tone and shape the future course, so contemplate them carefully with input from advisors.

We generally believe that canned press releases or attacks on the activist do not work. Today's capital markets are sophisticated about activism, and these tactics, along with ad hominem attacks or pro forma pledges of fidelity to shareholders, no longer help a company.

Moreover, tactics from a bygone era are usually received poorly by shareholders and likely will be counterproductive. Suing an investor, for example, is almost always a bad idea. Adopting a poison pill, changing advance notice provisions, or adopting last-minute bylaw changes to thwart a shareholder also generally backfire.

Shareholders now expect a substantive response to criticisms and suggestions. Respond to the shareholder on the merits.

Responses that work include the following:

- provide transparent, honest disclosures about the board's rationale for its decisions and actions;
- demonstrate recognition of performance challenges with a clear plan for fixing them; and
- show how value will be created with the current plan, capital structure, management, and incentives.

Careful analysis of your shareholder base can prove critical in knowing how to shape the message and win votes. Stock surveillance services can aid in watching trading to ensure that management knows where the stock is.

Finally, be sure to use the independent directors' voices, especially if there is a strong history of board self-refreshment and shareholder board support. Use a director to sit down with shareholders and explain strategy (and paths not taken), operational performance, executive pay plan design, and succession planning. Show the shareholders that the board is thinking actively about all of these critical areas and working hard on behalf of shareholders.

BE PROACTIVE AND VIGILANT

There's no doubt the past decade has seen enormous change in the relationship between shareholders, management teams, and boards. In this new era, more than ever, it is important for boards to be well composed, for companies to contemplate all value creation opportunities, and for all capital market actors to recognize that good ideas can originate both inside and outside the company.

Smart corporations take the lead, shaking up their own strategies, boards, governance, and engagement rules before activists force them to.

A DIRECTOR'S PERSPECTIVE

by Betsy Atkins

I have served as a public company director at more than a dozen companies. I have faced an activist investor approach at four of those companies, including from Starboard, Elliott Management, and JANA Partners.

The following are some important things I learned during these engagements:

Get help. Boards are accustomed to seeking specialized, independent assistance for executive compensation, cyber risk, and litigation. Get help from an outside specialist when an activist shows up. These are not legal problems or purely financial ones. Turn to someone who knows shareholders, communications, capital markets, activist techniques, and your company. At HD Supply, where I am lead director, we hired a firm to help us objectively review the activist's suggestions and perspective: it has proven enormously valuable.

Speak. Many activist investors will listen. At Polycom, we had an open and constructive dialogue with Elliott. We explained why we did not believe their suggestion was the best direction at that time. We ultimately sold the company and everyone was happy.

Listen. At Chico's (a clothing retailer), my co-author, Greg Taxin, was the activist. (That is where we met!) The board was initially very defensive and reluctant to acknowledge the performance issues at the company. Eventually, we were convinced and changed the board and the CEO. The company and stock then performed extremely well and was in the top 10 percent of all NYSE companies for four years.

Act. Activist investors are certainly not always right. But they also are rarely entirely wrong. Some have short-term horizons and recommendations that serve their own interests and not the interests of others. But activists are often well-informed, thoughtful and well-meaning. When you find such an activist, don't be afraid to embrace the "free" advice. Had the Darden board done so, perhaps they would not have experienced such an overwhelming rebuke from shareholders.

Adapted from Harvard Law School Forum on Corporate Governance and Financial Regulation, September 26, 2017.

KEY TAKE-AWAY

Boards must proactively try to avoid activist campaigns before they begin. A good way to start is by engaging a third party to review hot-button activist topics, such as board tenure, executive compensation, capital structure, and operational strategy.

Sources:

Bebchuk, Lucian A., et al. "The Long-Term Effects of Hedge Fund Activism," Harvard Law School John M. Olin Center Discussion Paper No. 802, SSRN, 7 Aug. 2013, www.ssrn.com.

Bebchuk, Lucian A., "The Myth that Insulating Boards Serves Long-Term Value," Columbia Law Review, Vol. 113, No. 6, pp. 1637-1694, October 2013, www.ssrn.com.

Strine, Leo E., "Who Bleeds When the Wolves Bite? A Flesh-and-Blood Perspective on Hedge Fund Activism and Our Strange Corporate Governance System," Yale Law Journal, Vol. 126, Pg. 1870, 2017, U of Penn, Inst for Law & Econ Research Paper No. 17-5, Harvard Law School, John M. Olin Institute for Law, Economics, and Business Discussion Paper no. 899, SSRN, 2 Feb. 2017, www.ssrn.com.

WE'VE SEEN TECH M&A BOOMS BEFORE—BUT SOMETHING IS DIFFERENT THIS TIME AROUND

By Betsy Atkins

A key role of the board is overseeing M&A. Technology M&A is having another record year and not showing any signs of slowing down. This year alone there have been 46 deals that were over $1 billion in value. While we've seen boom years in technology M&A before, something is different this time around.

The potential buyer universe has changed—the market has seen the rise of the new buyer types:

- Foreign acquirers, especially from China
- Cross-industry buyers
- Financial sponsors
- Institutional investors becoming active shareholders

To put this phenomenon in perspective, 73 percent of U.S.-based tech companies were sold to buyers who were either foreign, outside of the information technology industry, or a financial sponsor, which is a huge shift in the breadth of the buyer universe since 2014.

Importantly, of the 27 percent of transactions where the buyer was ultimately a U.S.-based technology company, a significant percentage had participation from foreign, non-technology, or financial sponsor buyers in the process who bid but didn't win. There is no doubt that the participation of these nontraditional buyers enhances the competitive tension of the process.

So why does this shift dramatically impact your board? We all know that board directors are subject to the duties of care. The issues a director will face during certain sale or merger transactions are subject to additional so-called Revlon duties to ensure that reasonable efforts are made to secure the highest price available. The carrying out of these duties is subject to intense scrutiny. It is a virtual certainty that an M&A transaction of a publicly listed company in the U.S. will ultimately lead to litigation focused on how the board conducted the process. So how do directors ensure they are getting the highest price available?

One of the most important things the board does when considering the sale of a company is selecting a financial advisor. Choosing a qualified, experienced financial advisor with relevant transaction capabilities who has knowledge of all the potential buyers will be one of the most important decisions you make.

Five years ago when the majority of deals were tech to tech, domestic to domestic, strategic to strategic, there were probably 68 great full-scale/full-reach advisors along with 810 great boutiques to consider for selling your company. Today, unless you are certain that your company doesn't appeal to the cross-industry or international or financial sponsor buyer, your smart choices are going to be fewer if you want to reach that broad buyer group and get the highest price consistent with your fiduciary duty.

So let's examine the trends that have impacted the M&A market in recent years and how this expanding universe of buyers in technology has shifted the board's advisory selection from boutique advisors to full-scale advisors with complete buyer reach access to maximize shareholder value.

FOREIGN BUYERS

In the past decade, inbound M&A activity of foreign companies buying U.S. companies has dramatically increased and is now a fifth of U.S. tech buyers. Geographies such as China have increased their outbound M&A transaction volume. In the first 6 months of 2016 alone, there were $42 billion China-announced outbound M&A transactions (see chart), including Ingram Micro's $6 billion sale to HNA Group's Tianjin Tianhai, which was the largest outbound acquisition by a Chinese company in the technology sector so far.

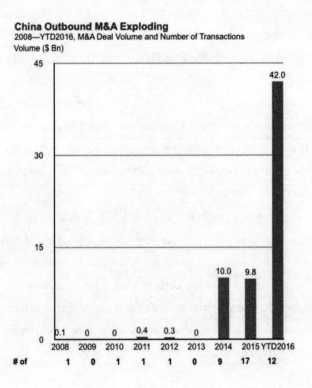

China Outbound M&A Exploding
2008—YTD2016, M&A Deal Volume and Number of Transactions
Volume ($ Bn)

	2008	2009	2010	2011	2012	2013	2014	2015	YTD2016
Volume	0.1	0	0	0.4	0.3	0	10.0	9.8	42.0
# of	1	0	1	1	1	0	9	17	12

Additionally, tax inversions, where targeted U.S. companies are re-domiciled abroad, have been increasingly common transaction structures attracting foreign buyers. Applied Materials' $9 billion merger with Tokyo Electron (which was later terminated due to antitrust concerns) was motivated in part by both companies' desire to lower corporate income taxes on future earnings through an inversion structure. The implication for the board of these transactions is clear: an effective financial advisor must have a global network with knowledge and access to potential buyers who will emerge from other geographies. That gives you a number of great choices but they need to be from among the global firms that have bankers around the globe with access to and knowledge of these interested foreign buyers.

CROSS-INDUSTRY BUYERS

Increasingly, buyers outside of your company's industry have emerged as competitive acquirers. In 2015 alone, there were $28.4 billion in cross-industry technology acquisitions, versus $10.8 billion in 2012. This is an amazing 263 percent increase in cross-industry buyer activity. Often it depends on your company's specific cross-industry appeal. A common theme has been cash-rich, mature buyers seeking new growth platforms to build on. Information technology provides lots of examples of nontraditional companies acquiring companies in technology, such as Monsanto's purchase of The Climate Corporation, Verizon's purchase of AOL and more recently Yahoo, and Walmart's acquisition of Jet. For these acquisitions to succeed, the financial advisor needs the ability to advise the board to include these cross-industry buyers in the sale process. Importantly, they need the relationships and knowledge to cultivate these new buyers who fall outside of tech. With 15 or so industries to cover, this leads us back to the larger firms that have access to the top buyers across industries, not just tech.

FINANCIAL SPONSOR BUYERS

Financial sponsors, or private equity firms, have become increasingly active.

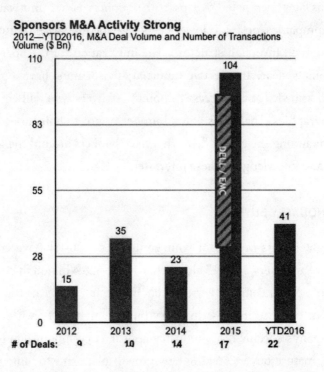

Sponsors M&A Activity Strong
2012—YTD2016, M&A Deal Volume and Number of Transactions
Volume ($ Bn)

Year	2012	2013	2014	2015	YTD2016
# of Deals:	9	10	14	17	22

To properly gauge the interest of financial sponsors and to advise the board if and when you should invite financial sponsors into a sale process, your financial advisor needs to have close relationships with the relevant financial sponsors. Most importantly, have the knowledge to assess their financial capacity to compete against strategic buyers and know the maximum amounts they can aggressively pay. A key component of credibility for directors in determining the sponsors' wherewithal comes from the financial advisor's leverage-lending expertise (both in the bank and bond markets), which are relied on to fund sponsor M&A transactions. Without real-time knowledge of the leveraged finance markets, your financial advisor will not be able to credibly determine the cost of financing that the sponsor relies on and, as a consequence, will not have the insights necessary to determine what price a financial sponsor could ultimately be able to pay. Several months ago, you would think okay, financial sponsors wouldn't pay 6.5x revenues and 69 percent premium for Cvent or 5.9x revenues and a 64 percent premium for Marketo, which Vista Equity Partners did earlier this year. Most recently, Infoblox was sold to a private equity firm at the highest premium ever paid by a financial sponsor for a technology company (73 percent).

Having in-depth knowledge of this market and the sponsor's financial capacity and desire is a critical component of the advice that financial advisors need to provide. We saw in the financial crisis of 2008 many of these financial sponsor-backed bids fall through; the consequences of misreading this market (guessing based upon prior deals instead of being in the leveraged finance market trading securities every day and knowing what is possible) can be devastating.

ACTIVIST SHAREHOLDERS

Although not typically a buyer of companies, activist shareholders are another player now impacting M&A transactions. Activist investing is not only the domain of a core group of hedge funds anymore; even institutional investors are becoming increasingly engaged. Of the campaigns announced in the last 12 months alone, about 86 separate investors have targeted more than 160 companies. Of these campaigns, 69 have led to activist additions to the board of directors, 21 have led to proxy fights, and 10 have resulted in sales of the target company. Many examples exist in technology of activists having direct involvement in situations that ultimately ended in the sale of a company—including my board, Polycom's, recently announced merger with Mitel, which later evolved into a sale of Polycom to Siris Capital. Having a financial advisor who has an experienced activism defense team is important in preparing the board early in building and articulating the company's long-term plan for value creation and helping the management and board understand their strategic landscape and M&A scenarios.

More M&A activity over the next year is likely due to continuing improvements in economic conditions, significant cash reserves, and investor pressure for increasing shareholder returns. M&A remains top of mind for directors. The factors that go into deciding the selection of your financial advisor should be carefully considered. Only an advisor with strong capabilities across all of the new emerging trends will enable you and your board to maximize value for your shareholders.

Adapted from Business Insider Online, November 2, 2016.

KEY TAKE-AWAY

M&A is changing with more nontraditional buyers, new financing sources, and activists entering into the mix. M&A review should be top of mind for board members trying to maximize value for their shareholders.

HOW TO MAKE COMPANY CULTURE MORE WELCOMING FOR WOMEN

By Betsy Atkins

Groups that nurture and empower their gender diversity gain in revenues and adaptability

In the past few weeks, attempts have been made to clean up the working environment at the ride-hailing company Uber. Former U.S. attorney-general Eric Holder was hired to investigate the group's culture. The chief executive, Travis Kalanick, has taken a leave of absence, and several new board members are on the job, including Arianna Huffington.

But these steps forward were followed by a step back when, at a meeting to unveil Mr. Holder's report, board member David Bonderman made a joke about women on the board. Mr. Bonderman later resigned.

I have served on the boards of many important tech companies, and this sounds to me like old news. Women seeking to advance their careers in the technology industry still find themselves bumping up against a silicon ceiling. Research from the Society of Women Engineers found that 20 percent of today's engineering school graduates are women, yet just 11 percent continue working in the field.[2] Women in IT leadership roles make up 12 percent of the total, according to a survey from Harvey Nash/KPMG.[3]

Changing any corporate culture is a challenge, but bringing diversity to the tech industry is even trickier. Fast-growth "unicorn" companies can quickly outgrow their founding, venture-based start-up corporate governance and can find themselves facing Uber-style crises. Yet in my experience, technology companies can and do nurture diverse, inclusive cultures.

There are several ways to do this. First, build internal career networks. At Volvo Car AB, where I serve on the board, we have launched a program in which I meet senior and mid-level women executives to discuss career development. We work with these executives to build on their strengths, clarify their career aspirations, and offer advice on advancement.

Second, make mentoring personal. On the board of Schneider Electric, I make a point of directly mentoring a number of women on the company's senior executive team. Women in management find it tremendously helpful to have someone in the boardroom who takes a personal interest in their career. Ms. Huffington will be in an ideal position to do this at Uber.

Third, go beyond mentoring. The tech industry, in particular, has too few role models for rising female talents. Companies should ask board members to sponsor female executives. There is a big difference between mentoring, best understood as periodic advice, and coaching or sponsoring, which involves more active help for individuals as they prepare to take the next step up in their careers. Women who are senior managers or board members can take mentoring up a notch by sponsoring women with high potential, taking personal ownership of career coaching for their top talents.

---

2   Nicholas St. Fleur, "Many Women Leave Engineering, Blame the Work Culture," NPR, 12 Aug. 2014, www.npr.org/sections/alltechconsidered/2014/08/12/339638726/many-women-leave-engineering-blame-the-work-culture.

3   The Harvey Nash/KPMG CIO SURVEY 2018,

Finally, recognize women making a difference. When I served as chair of the board's compensation committee at tech company Polycom, we were active in the annual recognition event for sales staff. I noted that women were leaders in sales—although they made up less than 10 percent of the sales force, they accounted for 34 percent of our President's Circle top sales performers. Making an added effort to celebrate this talent is crucial in sending the message that sales is not just a "guy thing." While Uber's woes make the news, they can also serve as a spark for making the support and advancement of women a boardroom mission. Talented women are a strategic asset to companies, and there is a growing body of research showing that groups that nurture gender diversity gain in revenue and adaptability. In any company, you cannot separate balance sheet results from corporate culture. When it comes to reshaping that culture to be more welcoming to women, the boardroom is the ideal place to start.

Adapted from Financial Times, June 19, 2017.

KEY TAKE-AWAY

Supporting the advancement of women in a company is a three-pronged effort that should including internal networking opportunities, mentoring, and high-level sponsorship of promising female executives.

AUTO INDUSTRY'S "BRO CULTURE" WAS ABLE TO CHANGE HOW THE AUTO INDUSTRY THINKS OF WOMEN

DIVERSITY LESSONS FOR SILICON VALLEY AND BEYOND FROM THE BIG THREE

By Betsy Atkins

They were the hot technology companies that helped shape America (and indeed, the world) by reinventing how we live and do business. However, these corporations grew to dominate their sectors with a powerful fuel—testosterone—building a powerful, clubby "bro culture" that shut women and minorities out of their executive and leadership ranks.

Silicon Valley? No, this rough-and-tumble culture was America's auto industry for most of its first century.

With the U.S. tech industry under fire for its poor diversity, sexist climate, and leadership insularity, we should realize that, long before there was an Uber or a Google, General Motors, Ford, and Chrysler were far more restrictive clubs, steeped in engineering and powerful economic engines.

Yet the Big Three broke up what once was the biggest good ol' boys' club. And how they did this can offer the "tech bros" and other bro-focused industries a lesson.

Automakers turned around their cultures through smart, strong leadership and tech diversity programs to become leaders in supporting and developing corporate women and minorities, in the corner offices and in the boardrooms.

GM today boasts an 18.1 percent black workforce, and its leadership ranks are 30 percent women and minorities. Global engineering-focused industrials, while still imperfect, are vastly more diverse than their "progressive" technology counterparts. Somehow the auto companies are seeking out and retaining the qualified STEM candidates who elude the Silicon Valley tech giants with their "who knows who" recruiting. Significantly, automakers have made strides in diversifying their leadership base.

Mary Barra's appointment as CEO and chairman of GM may be the most visible example of progress, but she is a natural evolution from the progress the automakers have made in developing their leadership pipeline.

GM corporate officers include several women, accounting for key operational and leadership positions. Women currently manage 6 of GM's 17 North American car plants under the stewardship of Alicia Boler Davis, who heads GM's global manufacturing. The automaker is also listed as a Diversity Inc. Top 50 Company for 2016 and 2017, something no tech company achieved in 2017.

"There's no doubt GM is the leader" for women in executive roles, says Mary Beth Vander Schaaf of *Automotive News*.

These values are seen in boardrooms as well. GM currently is approaching parity with 5 women board members out of 11. At Volvo Cars, 3 out of 13 board members are women, as are heads of software development, HR, and the legal department.

Ford has tapped Ken Washington, an African-American rocket scientist recruited from Lockheed Martin, as its chief technology officer and head of advanced engineering; and Ford Motor Credit Company is led by Joy Falotico.

Tellingly, Ford Motor Company recently named Marcy Klevorn, a veteran of the company's IT programs, to head its Smart Mobility Program, overseeing new ventures in ride-sharing, autonomous cars, and connected-car services. Klevorn reports directly to Ford CEO Jim Hackett.

Meanwhile, the tech industry, for all its flash and freshness, looks more like the pale male Detroit of the '50s when it comes to diversity. Tech industry titans such as Google struggle to improve their employee diversity beyond a largely white/Asian, male base (92 percent and 80 percent respectively at Google), with a shockingly poor representation among other racial minorities (only 1 percent of Google tech employees are African American).

No doubt the automakers have a century-long head start when it comes to improving their diversity.

- They have more evolved depth in their HR roles, which helps their organizational development and lets them look at the topic of diversity in a more thoughtful way.
- Plus, they gain the "compounding interest" benefit of women in their boardrooms and management chains. Women board members in my experience tend to be more active in mentoring and leaning in. With women in the boardroom reaching down, and women in the talent pipeline reaching up, Motown has shaped a winning formula.

How can this evolution away from bro culture in one industry have an impact on a much younger, still raucous one? The shared bridge is a coming, huge shift in personal mobility and the technology needed to achieve it.

Electric cars, autonomous vehicles, ride sharing, and "mobility as a service" are trends that both the old-line carmakers and new tech companies are struggling to master. The auto industry knows that it needs massive infusions of tech, coding talent, and fresh thinking (and cash) to lead in the evolution away from people driving their own cars. While tech companies may view the impending disruptions in the personal transportation industry as an opportunity to be exploited, the automakers know that adapting to that change is essential to their survival. And they know that ultimately the customers making the use decisions that will shape that industry will be much more diverse than the demographics of today's upper-echelon of Silicon Valley's wealth-generation machine.

Silicon Valley, meanwhile, is shaping the digital tools needed but is uncertain about how to move into the nuts and bolts of autos. Elon Musk's Tesla is currently struggling to turn itself into a profitable auto builder, GM invested $500 million in Lyft and acquired Cruise Automation, Ford invested in self-driving tech startup Argo, BWM is partnering with Intel, and dozens of other acquisitions, licensing plans, and joint ventures are in the works.

And who will be at the flash point when car builders and the techies join? Some of the strongest inroads by women in the auto industry have been at their digital functions. One of GM's recent moves has been to encourage the training and promotion of women in tech. It has made grants to groups like Code.org and Digital Promise for women coding education.

At all of the automakers, women have advanced most strongly in technical areas such as automated manufacturing, e-commerce, logistics and software design. It's no accident that GM, Ford, and Volvo have tapped women to lead their mobility efforts. Historically, marginalized groups have gained a head start in new technologies overlooked by the establishment. Women are finding that digital smarts are their fast track in an auto industry facing massive change. Could it be a myth that women and minorities don't have an interest in technology careers? Rather, they've "voted with their feet" to explore more friendly employment options.

The tech companies can look to some of the automakers' efforts investing in pipelines and recruiting at a wide and diverse landscape of educational institutions, mentoring, and rotational and training programs. These expand the experience and worldview of its employees. Perhaps the tech industry should push their definition of "employee-friendly retention policies" beyond fro-yo machines and ping pong tables in bolstering their own diversity efforts.

This also means that the frat-house culture of some hot tech firms faces a rude wakeup call when they make the linkages with automakers they'll need in future. Instead of metal-bending guys in suits, the techies may encounter smart, executive women who know as much as they do about crunching code.

Better still, the dudes will discover a diverse role model for their industrial future.

Adapted from Directors & Boards, September 22, 2017.

KEY TAKE-AWAY

Silicon Valley tech companies have a lot to learn from the automakers in terms of supporting women leaders and expanding diversity in their leadership. Diversity is critical to building long-term company value.

HOW DOES YOUR COMPANY SCORE ON TECH RESILIENCE?

By Betsy Atkins

All boards now know they need to have a cyber oversight review annually at a minimum.

Many of the formats have converged on the NIST (National Institute of Standards and Technology) one-page scorecard, which lists 22 items broken down into 5 function categories. Each of the 22 items is a short bulleted statement addressing different aspects of cyber readiness so that the board can provide a review to ensure that the company is investing properly, has the right manpower inside, or has established relationships with external services to keep the company's intellectual property and key information protected from cyberattack. That review results in a status for each category: red—absent; yellow—partial; and green—compliant. If the category isn't green, then a plan of action may be put into place to get to green status.

The far bigger risk companies now need to look at is tech-enabled resilience. Companies are no longer simply product or services companies. To remain competitive, every company is a tech-enabled product or a tech-enabled service company. Therefore, the scorecard that I suggest every board use is a tech-enablement focused NIST-style scorecard.

The way a company could look at doing this would be to create a similar framework to NIST. I have created a sample scorecard to look at with five functions to be reviewed with more detailed categories in each. Below is my suggested scorecard with proposed functions and categories.

Tech Resilience Score Card

Function	Category	Tech Resilience		
		Compliant	Partial	Absent
Customer Engagement	The company website is current and customers can have an omnichannel experience when engaging in either B2B or B2C transactions starting on a mobile phone to a tablet to a PC.			
	The number of clicks required in order to engage with the website is competitive with peers or better.			
	The products or services are designed for mobile first engagement.			
	Customers are able to transact in a frictionless way to buy our product or service.			
	We have social media policies in place that reflect our brand.			
Use of Artificial Intelligence/machine Learning	We use business intelligence, AI and machine learning analytics to identify the highest profit products or services.			
	We regularly review our SKUs and trim down the ones that do not contribute at the right gross margin.			
	We use machine learning and AI to assemble offers and bundles in a way that maximizes upsell and revenue.			
	We use AI and machine learning algorithms to identify our most valuable customers.			
	We use AI and machine learning to identify and product turn/cancellation/dissatisfaction.			

HOW DOES YOUR COMPANY SCORE ON TECH RESILIENCE?

Function	Category	Tech Resilience		
		Compliant	Partial	Absent
Training and Forward Building	We regularly invest in tech training for our product development, for example do we use PluralSite online training courses.			
	We do company wide regular online training for cyber security compliance.			
	We do online training for anti-harassment training using gamification to drive engagement.			
	We track the number of ERP systems we have and have a plan to merge them.			
	We encourage and measure the amount of usage of our company intranet.			
	We use regularly use video for meetings.			
Adoption of New Technology	Is your technology ready for the wireless 5G revolution that will take hold in 2019?			
	Have we assessed the impact of Google Duplex on our business? Google Duplex is an A.I. phone system that adjusts to the person, instead of the person adjusting to the system, including natural voice patterns, the ability to elaborate and adjust to interruptions.			
	We use Agile development tools and services like Docker Containers.			
	We have considered the impact of same day delivery that has become the norm and expectation for products and service.			
	We have IoT sensor enablement on our products and services.			
	We evaluate new macro trends like robotic process automation and assess how we might use it.			
	We evaluate new product trends like crypto blockchain technology.			
Tech Partnering	We have outside cyber penetration testing on a regular basis.			
	We use outsourced product development services to augment our internal capabilities.			
	If our business portals are focused on social media networks (Facebook) have we expanded to other outlets as social media use is expected to decline.			
	We have co-innovation partnerships with unique high value startups.			
	We have outside, third party reviews of our business model and our go to market to look at macro trends like the sharing economy, the gig economy, engaging millennials, marketplaces, and Klout influence scores.			

139

BE BOARD READY

Proactively reviewing your company's tech enablement and digital transformation could be a twice-a-year exercise due to the velocity of change in technology. I suggest this review be part of the annual offsite board meeting that focuses on future strategy.

KEY TAKE-AWAY

Tech resilience is the key to company survival. All companies are now tech companies, and ensuring you remain current is a basic ERM function. Using a scorecard will help you assess, review, and take action to update your company's technology.

BOARDS AND RANSOMWARE: DEALING WITH THE DEVIL

By Betsy Atkins

For all the clever coding involved, most ransomware delivers a very crude but deadly message when it strikes your company. Important company files are locked, and may be destroyed, unless you pay a specific ransom amount, anonymously, within a short deadline. At that point, the panic sets in. But if your top management, IT team, and board of directors have devoted some time, thought, and resources in advance, you'll know how to respond (and might dodge the bullet altogether).

In my own recent boardroom experience, how boards should deal with cybersecurity is one of the hottest topics. I've been an evangelist for getting boards active in setting and assuring effective corporate digital policies. Much of this should be basic good governance for the 21st century. Realize that a cyberattack is now a matter of when, not if. Make your board digitally savvy so that it can ask smart questions on technology, threats, and liabilities. Assure things like up-to-date platforms, software, and third-party testing.

I should note that the majority of company hacking attacks still involves these conventional threats—the cyber equivalent of smash-and-grab theft. However, the special dangers posed by digital hostage-taking demand a unique corporate governance role. If regular hackers penetrate your systems to steal money or data, there are few shades of grey. There may be debates between IT and the rest of management on budgeting for safeguards (the board should be IT's advocate and "nudger" on this, by the way). However, the priorities after a conventional breach are never in doubt—assess and limit the damages, and learn from the attack.

HOW RANSOMWARE IS DIFFERENT

Ransomware is existentially different, and goes to the heart of a board's governance and fiduciary role. Do we as a company pay a ransom demand, or do we take the moral high ground and say no? Your board needs to tackle this question, with its uncomfortable blend of technology and ethics, now, before an attack. The major ransomware strains, such as Petya and WannaCry, offer a short time frame (sometimes as little as 24 hours) to pay up or face the consequences. Convening a board meeting that quickly to deal with a flash crisis would be both impractical and unwise. Further, the actual ransom itself can be oddly small. Would you really convene an emergency board session to discuss expending $1,000?

Real-world board experiences with ransomware suggest a better way. I've seen ransom demands firsthand at one of my boards. And I've spoken with Bill Lenehan, CEO of Four Corners Property Trust, who's also faced these traumas. Here are some board ideas specifically targeted at dealing with the unique threat of a ransomware attack:

Get your ethical discussion out of the way now. Your top executives and IT staff need guidance from the boardroom on the big question of whether or not the company should submit. The call is not an easy one. Losing business (and perhaps the business itself) by taking the moral high ground is not your call as a shareholder fiduciary. Your number-one mission is to protect the business for investors. That may involve the tough decision to pay up if it will save data or needed access.

"Boards need to provide guidance and support on how this is handled," recalls Bill Lenehan. He finds laying out the issues directly to the board helps clarify their thinking. "I was talking with a 70-year-old board chair, and said, 'Let me throw you a curve. You're trying to close a $200 million acquisition, when suddenly your employees get a ransomware demand for a total of $3,000. If you don't pay, you jeopardize the deal, your relationship with numerous counter-parties, and maybe the company itself.' The response? 'My God, I never thought of this!'"

WHY YOUR BOARD SHOULD BE CONCERNED

Hold this debate now at the board level, because when a hacker's WARNING screen pops up, it's too late for philosophy.

Shape a corporate ransomware policy based on this discussion. Take the strategic principles the board has developed and turn them into a working tactical policy. Include functional steps, like who is to be notified, who makes the final payment decision, damage/cost tradeoffs to weigh, etc. Also, will you even be able to pay the crooks? It sounds distasteful, but assure that you have the mechanisms in place to quickly meet the ransom demands if you choose to.

"You don't want to be scrambling to pay, figuring out how to practically make this work," Bill Lenehan recalls from his own experience as CEO of Four Corners Property Trust. At 5:30 one morning, he received a text message from the company controller telling him there was a problem—a short-term ransomware attack was spreading globally. "Our board chairman was out of the country, hours behind us, so what do I do as CEO? Would I pay, or not pay, do I even need to inform my board, or just hurry to set up a bitcoin account?"

The CEO and other staff should not have to make these decisions on the fly—and if they do, it's the fault of the board, which didn't prepare in time. "Ransomware is not the fault of the CEO," notes Lenehan. "It's like a school snow day—you have to set your decision policies in advance." (Lenehan also notes that his small company has a staff of 12 and is as far off the business news radar as can be—yet hackers still found them.)

No policy can mean inability to respond at all. At a major company whose board I serve, we faced a short-term ransomware demand and decided we had to pay. But the hackers demanded payment in bitcoin, and the company didn't have a bitcoin account. This took two days to set up—by which time the deadline had passed. Also, ask what you'll do if other problems crop up. In Europe, a recent Petya attack demanded payment to the bit-napper's Posteo email account. But before the victims could comply, Posteo had blocked the mailbox.

Ransomware is not just an internal danger. Even after you shape a sound emergency policy for your corporate response, what about the suppliers, customers, and advisors you depend on? Lenehan tells of a ransomware strike, not at his company, but at a major law firm they were depending on to close a $20 million acquisition. "The lawyers got an email from IT early in the morning telling everyone to not turn on their laptops and to check them in immediately." A pending deal was suddenly frozen solid.

HOW TO DEFEND YOUR ORGANIZATION

What would happen at this very moment if one of your top vendor's or client's IT system instantly went dark for an uncertain period of time? Are they able to back up their information with systems completely walled off from the afflicted ones?

Fight hackers with unconventional warfare. Above, I noted the generic things a board can do to improve the technical odds of avoiding and fighting cyber mischief. Push IT to innovate outside its normal comfort zone. Third-party vendors like Optiv, SecureWorks, and Stroz specialize in penetration testing, 24/7 threat monitoring, and ethical hacking. Your IT staff says they have the latest software updates and threat assessments? Good—let's contract with outside experts who can make sure. The expenses involved should be modest, and today they are a basic cost of doing business. Want to drive a car? You need to buy insurance. Want to operate in today's digital world? Invest in outside cyber expertise.

Speaking of insurance, check your liability and other business policies when it comes to hacking damages, and specifically ransomware costs. What sort of losses are covered, which aren't, how much could ransomware losses total, what compliance measures must you have in place, and what are disqualifiers? Also, how should your company decide on making a claim? (If you file a claim for a ransomware payment of $5,000, will your premiums shoot up by ten times that amount?) "If someone demands $350 in bitcoin, it may be like when someone keys your car in a parking lot," notes Lenehan. "Rather than making a claim, you just get it detailed out on your own dime."

Ultimately, boards and management need to respond to a ransomware crisis the same way they respond to any company crisis. They must assure that good response tools and plans are in place and functioning, that tough questions are asked, and that everyone knows their role. But for the board, ransomware prep demands an added step—asking yourself if you're ready to deal with the devil.

Adapted from Diligent, August 21, 2107.

KEY TAKE-AWAY

Ransomware is a special kind of hacking that the board should have reviewed and created a policy and procedure in advance, including opening a bitcoin account.

INSIDE THE BOARDROOM: FOSTERING DIVERSITY, MITIGATING CYBER RISKS, AND MORE

By Betsy Atkins

(In this edition of "Inside the Boardroom," I answered readers' questions about inclusiveness and diversity, data breaches and cyber threats, and institutional investors.)

How can boards help foster inclusiveness and diversity? What should we be doing to avoid the type of sexism and discrimination that allegedly occurred at Uber and elsewhere?

Boards can help oversee the tone at the top of a company to ensure there is active oversight to avoid sexism or discrimination. Boards may want to review hiring goals for gender diversity and minorities. Also, with the CEO's support, board members who have a passion for or connection to the topic of inclusiveness and diversity can offer to both mentor and meet with groups within the company.

At Volvo, I host a luncheon meeting a few times each year for female middle-management and high-potential executives. Male board members can also actively mentor and sponsor women and minority employees to foster inclusiveness. The board can discuss if they think it is helpful to proactively ensure the company has a wide range of abilities, experience, knowledge and strengths.

In the wake of the recent data breach suffered by Equifax, it's becoming clear that reducing vulnerability to cyber threats is increasingly critical. What is the role of the board in terms of cybersecurity oversight? What can directors do to stay informed about the issue and take appropriate precautionary measures?

Cyber breach is one of the key vulnerabilities that boards review as part of their enterprise risk-management oversight and is frequently a priority on the audit committee's annual calendar. The impact of a cybersecurity breach extends far beyond costs and losses related to the data that is stolen, impacting brand reputation and consumer and investor confidence. This, in my view, elevates the risk and the need for board attention.

Directors may want to invite the chief information officer or chief information security officer to present the company's prevention, detection, and mitigation policies and programs to the full board annually, perhaps at a working dinner. Additionally, particularly given the Equifax breach, it is critical to understand the company's data policies regarding software updates and patches as part of an overall compliance program. Another practice to consider is inviting an outside expert—such as a representative from a cybersecurity company like SecureWorks, the Chertoff Group, or FireEye—to speak to the board as part of its ongoing education. Finally, at a minimum, boards should ask if there is a standard cyber risk matrix that they can look at, such as the NIST Dashboard.

What changes have you observed in how the board engages with institutional investors? What practices should boards consider adopting to build institutional investor relations?

There is a significant emerging trend for boards to meet with their large institutional investors—such as big index funds like Vanguard, State Street, and Fidelity. There are two groups within these index funds: the investment group and the governance group. The governance group will vote the proxy either in support or against management's recommendations on pay, equity grants as part of compensation to leadership and management, and, importantly, any response to activist proxy proposals.

Meeting with the governance group on an annual basis is a good way to build relationships and credibility for questions and concerns that inevitably come up related to compensation packages—specifically CEO and senior executive salaries, bonuses, and long-term incentive equity grants—and activist proposals. The investment group is typically on a quarterly update cycle with the company via the CFO and investor relations team. The board does not normally meet with the investor group. The lead director on one of my public boards has been meeting with both individual active investment funds and the index funds' governance groups for the past three years. These meetings have proven critical to gaining their support on the issues mentioned above. I recommend this as a new best practice for boards to consider and discuss.

Adapted from Board Member, Fourth Quarter 2017.

KEY TAKE-AWAY

Boards can dive more deeply into topics like diversity, cyber threats, and institutional investor engagement.

BETSY ATKINS TALKS TO ARTHUR LEVITT ABOUT THE CURRENT STATE OF BOARDS

How should boards deal with sexual harassment issues? What is the best way to protect a company from cybersecurity threats? What is it really going to take to improve diversity in the boardroom? Why does every company need a digital director and a tech committee?

(During a wide-ranging and informative interview, Bloomberg Radio host and former SEC Chairman Arthur Levitt and I discussed these important topics, and more. The entire interview was divided into three separate articles. Part 1 is presented below.)

Arthur Levitt: You have spent decades on multiple boards. What is the current state of boards? Are most boards still stuck in the past, or are they evolving with the times?

Betsy Atkins: Boards are evolving with the times, but not quickly enough. Velocity of change has not totally permeated the boardroom. Boards are still heavily focused on a one-year lens with a quarterly operational focus, versus a longer-term horizon of understanding the rapidly changing competitive landscape and the need of the company to stay contemporary and vibrant for the future.

AL: What will be the big issues for boards during 2018?

BA: There are two ways to answer that: There are the corporate governance watchdog issues of institutional shareholder services, such as board committees, refreshment, diversity, and ESG (environmental, social, and governance) issues. However, I think the bigger and more important issue for corporate boards is going to be "the business of the business." Failing to employ new technologies and new business models to keep companies competitive is a bigger threat to the well-being of a business than corporate hygiene governance issues.

Companies underperform when they don't remain vibrant and contemporary. The big issues are understanding new business models like the eBay (Nasdaq: EBAY) marketplace and how that applies to other businesses; or the sharing economy where you see Airbnb emerge; or the rise of the gig economy, which has employees working "gigs" as opposed to full-time corporate jobs. Boards need to examine how to employ machine learning and AI to replicate highly paid white-collar employees in traditional industries like insurance. The biggest threat is that a company slowly melts while new interlopers capture their market share.

AL: How would you counsel boards to deal with the issue of sexual harassment both in resolving potential current issues and how to move forward? What kind of crisis plan would you recommend boards consider?

BA: Boards are responsible for oversight of tone at the top, compliance training, and the escalation process. The values and code of conduct of the company are exemplified by the full leadership team. Most companies have mechanisms in place to escalate issues, including hotlines to the audit committee, the chief human resource officer, or the general counsel. When a potential issue is raised, the board needs to own it quickly, conduct a rapid first-pass review to determine if a serious problem exists, and then make a business decision whether or not to conduct a broader investigation.

One mistake many boards make is to abdicate that first-pass review to their outside law firm instead of using a firm that specializes in background checks and investigations. Outside law firms are slower, more expensive, and they typically subcontract out those internal investigations.

AL: 145 million Americans had their data breached at Equifax. Did this rattle companies about cybersecurity threats, and is this the biggest issue for boards now?

BA: Cybersecurity breach is inevitable. Boards need to understand that statistically, every company has already been breached. The relevant question to ask is, what is the board's cyber oversight practice?

Boards should utilize standard measures such as the National Institute of Standards and Technology framework of 22 computer security items. The company should conduct regular, unscheduled penetration testing, and ensure that critical intellectual property is segmented and protected. For example, if a pharmaceutical company is developing a new blockbuster drug, it's critical to shareholders that data related to the new molecule compound is segregated and has special protection. Companies should implement appropriate training so that employees don't respond to phishing. Large companies should also have an independent, third-party cyber monitoring service.

Corporations also need standing tech committees, versus overloading their audit committees. Cyber is a forward-looking threat, while most audit functions are forensic and backward-looking.

However, cyber threats are not the biggest issue for boards now. The biggest issue is that the company continuously evolves to remain contemporary, innovative, and competitive.

AL: At HD Supply, where you are on the board, the company did a review of cyber threats. What did you find and what did management do?

BA: HD does very serious cyber oversight and brings in external cyber experts to educate the board. HD also has the chief information security officer present to the board annually and the company leans in to be sure we have proper training of our employees against phishing, which is the biggest vulnerability. With Distributed Denial of Service (DDoS) ransomware attacks gaining prevalence, we took the step to adopt a ransomware policy and we opened a bitcoin account so that we would be able to decrypt files if we had a DDoS attack.

AL: Betsy, you advise that these days, all boards need a digital director. What is this?

BA: A digital director has broad technology experience in tech realms such as large enterprise software systems, on-premise software and cloud computing, mobile, social media, machine learning, AI, and cyber. More importantly, good digital directors bring understanding of innovation methodologies, such as distributed agile development; new business models, such as online marketplaces; gig economies, such as TaskRabbit and Thumbtack; and shared-economy ownership models, such as Uber and Airbnb.

Digital competency is not covered by just one tech silo, so boards need at least one, but preferably two or three, digital directors due to the velocity of change.

AL: On February 20, the SEC voted to force companies to disclose cyber-attacks. The Securities and Exchange Commission's new guidance says that companies should inform investors about cybersecurity risks, even if they have not yet been targeted by hackers in a cyberattack. It also stresses that companies publicly disclose breaches in a timely fashion, and instructs firms to take steps to prevent executives and others with previous knowledge of a breach from trading in its securities before the information is made public.

BA: The SEC guidance on cybersecurity disclosure is sensible. The market will reward or punish companies that do or don't disclose. We must be mindful of the impact of over-regulation, which you can see as Sarbanes Oxley has impacted the number of IPOs. Before SOX, there were an average 528 IPOs a year. Since it was enacted, an unintended consequence is that number has fallen to 135, a decline of nearly 75 percent.

AL: Where should responsibility rest for cybersecurity: with the audit committee and board, with congress, or with regulators?

BA: Cybersecurity oversight should rest with the board, under the purview of a newly created tech committee—audit committees are too busy. The free market will reward or punish companies that are not careful with data patching, current cyber protection, and breach mitigation. Corporations have a huge economic incentive to protect their brand with consumers and to protect their most valuable intellectual properties.

KEY TAKE-AWAY

The velocity of change in business today requires that corporate boards stay current on new business models, incorporate technology into their strategy, and keep up on cybersecurity.

THINKING OUTSIDE THE AUDIT COMMITTEE BOX: A BETTER WAY TO MANAGE RISK

By Betsy Atkins

An ever-increasing reliance on evolving technologies has left corporations vulnerable to cyberattack and business model disruption. At the same time, enterprise risk management has landed squarely in the sights of institutional investors. As a result, boards must enhance their oversight of risk management.

Audit committee members, who have had responsibility for risk management on many boards, are feeling strained as regulatory demands intersect with that increased responsibility; in a recent survey of nearly 1,500 audit committee members by KPMG, half of those surveyed reported that their committees may not have the time or expertise needed to be effective in all areas of responsibility.

Thus, there is a growing awareness that boards may need to evolve, including by altering board committee structures and reallocating workflows.

This article outlines some of my expertise regarding effective oversight of risk management in the boardroom in a question-and-answer format.

Q: What is a board's primary role with respect to enterprise risk management?

A: The board's primary roles related to enterprise risk management are ensuring that the company's strategy is still relevant, examining the real risks the company faces, and determining what risk oversight mechanisms are most effective. The lifecycle of S&P 500 companies has declined from about 60 years in 1958 to below 20 years now, begging the question, why do so many established public companies go out of business?

...as a result, the average lifespan of a S&P500 company is now less than 20 years, from c60 years in the 1950s

Source: Credit Suisse

While some get acquired, go private, or become bankrupt, too many disappear because they don't innovate or stay relevant. The rate of change in business today is alarming. A very real threat for the shareholders is that a company quietly loses market share for three or four years and then suddenly wakes up to realize they've lost nearly 30 percent of their market. When that happens, we see Blockbuster and Borders get replaced on the S&P 500 by Netflix and Amazon. Both of those companies might still be in business if their boards had been keeping an eye on new business models, digitally born companies, and marketplace disrupters.

Q: What are some strategies boards can employ to better manage risk?

A: There are a number of tactics for load-leveling the risk management responsibility across a board, including:

1. SEPARATING THE OVERSIGHT OF FUTURE-LOOKING RISKS FROM BACKWARD-LOOKING RISKS.

Divide risks into two main categories: backward-looking risks and future-looking risks. Forensic, backward-looking risks include financial internal controls, review of quarterly financial statements, and compliance with FASB regulations. These are historically—and appropriately—the strength and domain of the audit committee.

Future (and emerging) risks include cyberattacks, cyber breaches that damage brands, disrupted business models, and emerging digital marketplaces. Technology risk, too, needs to be examined. Although disaster recovery has long been a purview of the audit committee, oversight of cybersecurity and technology risks do not necessarily belong on the audit committee agenda.

2. ASSIGNING OVERSIGHT OF FORWARD-LOOKING RISKS TO THE GOVERNANCE COMMITTEE.

Audit committees are disproportionately busy on corporate boards. Compensation committees are also quite busy during certain times of the year, leaving governance and nominating committees as the least busy.

The nominating mandate is clear and happens in short bursts: refresh and renew the board. But what is governance on behalf of shareholders? Often, it's limited to code of conduct, tone at the top, and preventing foreign corrupt illegal practices and sexually predatory behavior. However, governance really ought to be ensuring—on behalf of the shareholders—that the company is relevant, innovative, and vibrant.

I chair the nominating and corporate governance committee on the board of HD Supply. Our audit committee looks at internal controls, financial reporting, and other functions that audit committees historically have performed. We created a more future-looking role for the nominating and governance committee to look at business strategy, including the digital transformation of the company's business. We've had outside speakers from major consultancies, such as McKinsey, Boston Consulting Group, and Accenture, come in and educate us. We're also working with artificial intelligence experts who can help us understand how to apply that technology to increase B2B sales revenue.

3. INCORPORATING WORKING SESSIONS INTO BOARD MEETINGS.

Like other boards, at HD Supply we have a nominating and corporate governance, audit, and compensation committee readout. But what's a little different from other boards I've served on is that we have a lively discussion around the board table during these readouts, regularly debating our major initiatives of digital and business model transformation.

And we believe in working board dinners, held at our headquarters in the training center versus at a restaurant. We bring in the company's senior leadership team, as well as contemporary and knowledgeable external speakers, to discuss topics we want to immerse ourselves in.

4. LEVERAGING TECHNOLOGY TO MANAGE RISKS BY MONITORING CORPORATE HEALTH.

There are a number of metrics that should be tracked to assess corporate health and flush out potential risk factors; these are related to compliance, digital advancement, product and service development pipelines, market share, customer satisfaction, and employee turnover.

There are companies and platforms out there, such as Boardvantage, that can capture and track those types of metrics to develop an automated corporate health dashboard. Are we as digitally advanced as Amazon? Are we developing and introducing new products and services as quickly as Lowe's? Are we an innovation leader, laggard, or fast follower? Are we growing market share or losing it? Are we using artificial intelligence as effectively as our competitors? These are the benchmarks we want to monitor.

5. VIEWING BOARD COMPOSITION AS A COMPETITIVE ASSET.

It is incumbent on boards to consider, and actively discuss on the governance committee, whether the board should be viewed as a competitive asset to the shareholders or just fiduciaries who do oversight. If the determination is to be a competitive asset, then the board really ought to look at the competencies around the table the same way a company looks at its management leadership team.

Boards ought to carefully consider, given the turbulent sea of changes that businesses are navigating, how best to refresh and bring on a director or two with skill sets they'll need in the next three to five years. Boards should appoint members the same way corporations hire, rather than waiting passively for a retirement to free a seat at the table.

By employing these tactics, boards can better fulfill a critical governance mandate: identify business-killing risks before it's too late.

Adapted from Governance Clearinghouse, May 2017.

KEY TAKE-AWAY

Consider moving forward-looking risk management (such as cyberattacks, cyber breaches, disruptive business models, and technology risk) to the governance committee.

HOW THE BOARD SHOULD FACE UP TO FACEBOOK'S ISSUES

By Betsy Atkins

The job of Facebook's board is to oversee the company for long-term growth and profitability. Part of the directors' job is anticipating risks and looking forward to future-proof the company as the market and regulatory environment evolves.

The first big regulatory reform to hit Facebook was Europe's GDPR. These new regulations protect users' data so that it can't be mined and sold to companies such as Cambridge Analytica who then sell their individual data to political campaigns.

There are big issues now facing the Facebook board. The first one is transparency and information from management to the board. The New York Times expose[4] showed Sandberg and Zuckerberg's denial and suppression of major business risks from Chief Security Officer Alex Stamos when he attempted to investigate the Russia situation.

---

4   Frenkel, Sheera, et al. "Delay, Deny and Deflect: How Facebook's Leaders Fought Through Crisis." *The New York Times*, 14 Nov. 2018, www.nytimes.com/2018/11/14/technology/facebook-data-russia-election-racism.html.

Boards must be able to rely on their management team's honesty and transparency to share major corporate risks. The board should take this opportunity to redefine and refresh the line between what topics come to the board and which ones do not bubble up.

This leads to the bigger topic of revisiting the definition of the company's business.

Is Facebook a social media lifestyle engagement platform? Yes, 68 percent of U.S. adults use Facebook.

Is Facebook an e-commerce platform? Yes, Facebook's platform, Facebook Store, allows sellers to list products for sale and set up a shopping cart to connect payments. Their new Instagram Shopping app is reportedly targeting $4 billion in sales by 2020.

Is Facebook a digital advertising platform? Yes, the company earned $34 billion in worldwide advertising revenue in 2018.

Is Facebook a data mining/business intelligence platform? Yes, this was clearly shown by the Cambridge Analytica scandal where they sold data on 87 million users.

Is Facebook a news "media" platform? Yes, a media company is an intervening agency, means or instrument. Facebook provides news via member posting and they partner with the New York Times, Buzzfeed, and NBC for content.

My belief is that the board's oversight duty includes challenging management to refine, refresh, and, when needed, redefine the scope and definition of their company's businesses. Accidental drift/gradual metamorphosis is not the best company strategy and is not effective board oversight. Facebook has gradually evolved into many specific and intermingled business lines.

This is not an unusual phenomenon in the world of platform dominance. We see this at Amazon with their original Kindle business building into an e-commerce leader and adding their analogous Amazon Stores and AWS cloud services.

The different issue at Facebook is that they have crossed over into being a media company and have not directly forced this issue and the compliance requirements of being a media company. According to Oxford Dictionary, the definition of a media company is a company that provides broadcasting, film, and internet services.

Facebook can't defend with honesty that they are only a social media platform company when 43 percent of U.S. adults get their news from Facebook, according to Pew Research.[5]

The board would best serve the shareholders to ask management to assess the risk and trade-offs of the cost of proactively embracing the regulatory framework of being a media company.

- What revenue streams would Facebook lose?
- Would Facebook lose the revenue stream of Russian placements? Not necessarily. Just as with newspapers and magazines, they would simply identify the placement as a "special advertising section."

The reputational risk and downside of not addressing the known hate posts to drive violence, the known political purchase to produce biased manipulation, or the clearly false information will have consequences, and the public will demand that regulators step in.

Transparency and authenticity with users and consumers will serve Facebook. Look at how Starbucks faced the issue of racial bias. By addressing this, it helped their brand. It's not believable that Facebook—whose entire monetization model is based on tracking every user's clicks, cookies, eyeball duration of engagement to create a unique segment for targeted ads and mined data—can claim ignorance or innocence on posted information. It's a silly and insulting assertion.

---

5   John Gramlich, "8 Facts about Americans and Facebook," *Pew Research Center*, 24 Oct. 2018, www.pewresearch.org/fact-tank/2018/10/24/facts-about-americans-and-facebook/.

We all want Facebook to thrive and accept that they make money via digital advertising. To make their ads valuable, they need maximized eyeballs, engagement, and on-site time to charge more. TV, newspapers, and magazines report subscription numbers to attract their advertisers. That's why the newspaper and TV adage of "if it bleeds, it leads" is true. They are rewarded to drive viewership.

TV media has their Neilsen ratings to confirm that the eyeballs on the screen/number of watchers is accurate. Facebook has an inherent conflict of interest in self-reporting their numbers of users and level of engagement, but that's a matter the marketplace will correct over time.

Ultimately, Facebook will need to be regarded as an online news media outlet. My view is that their board should proactively discuss with management the pros, cons, risks, and business case trade-offs. Generally, it's better to have a thoughtful strategy and to embrace the inevitable.

This flags the final big Facebook board governance elephant in the room. When you have a dynamic founder who is both CEO and chairman, it's hard for there to be transparency for the board into management issues.

Mark Zuckerberg has 16 percent ownership, but the big issue is his super-voting rights of 60 percent control of the voting shares. The shareholders will want their board to represent and be able to stress test and challenge management's logic. That's the essence of the board's role: to make business judgments for *all* shareholders.

Perhaps it's time for Mark Zuckerberg to look to the model of Microsoft or Intel where their founders, Bill Gates and Andy Grove, separated the chairman and CEO role. This latest set of Facebook missteps highlights two big issues for Facebook and the Board:

1. Should the chairman role be separated when the CEO has 60 percent voting rights?

2. Should the Facebook board challenge management to present the business case for embracing a balanced media regulatory framework?

Ultimately, the shareholders and the marketplace will decide the issues!

Adapted from Forbes, November 16, 2018.

KEY TAKE-AWAY

Facebook's board should review the possibility of embracing regulation ahead of being forced to do so. They should also consider separating the chairman and CEO roles in order to ensure that the board is getting full information on risks.

BOARDS NEED A SOCIAL MEDIA STRATEGY FOR CRISIS MANAGEMENT

By Betsy Atkins

Boards have historically used the standard enterprise risk management approach for dealing with crisis. ERM was overseen by the audit committee. Typically ERM looked at things such as disaster recovery from hurricanes and expanded to oversee areas such as cyber readiness.

While these topics need to be covered, I think the real risk is the fact that we live in the age of social media and a 45-second response to mitigate corporate crisis is what is really required to preserve the company's brand and engage appropriately with investors, customers, and employees in the community.

In the old ERM format, the board would list the ten most likely crises a company would face. For example, if you're a restaurant, the ten terrible crises you have to have a response for could include food poisoning, #MeToo issues, kidnapping, breach of customer info, armed attack/active shooter, etc.

In today's world I think boards who perform their ERM and risk mitigation oversight should challenge management teams to have a pre-reviewed "on the shelf" social media response ready to go for the ten most likely risks.

Look at the difference between Starbucks's speedy response on an alleged racial bias issue and contrast that with the flat-footed response of United Airlines's passenger abuse removal scandal followed by the puppy suffocation death.

A social media response must have genuine authenticity and truly resonate as coming from the heart. A social media response needs to be pre-thought out and ready to be instantly deployed. The actual issue may not be one of the ten that management has figured out, but it will certainly be a variant. This exercise will enable management and the board to have a plan that they can deploy instantly.

Additionally, traditional PR and IR firms are not experts at social media. A boutique social media firm should be part of all public corporations' contracted resources. Just as you have an accounting firm, a law firm and a PR firm, so too you need a social media firm.

A dedicated social media firm has a unique network of relationships to get your message out there. Your in-house social media will never be adequate or as deeply wired in as a dedicated external social media firm.

To be impactful as directors, we need to look out for the risks that will either harm our brand equity or enhance our company. It is the chance for the company to have their Tylenol tampering moment where the incident shows that the CEO and company truly care about the consumer.

This is a valuable exercise boards should consider incorporating.

Adapted from Forbes, November 2, 2018.

KEY TAKE-AWAY

Companies should have a list of 10 prepared and board-approved social media responses to the most likely issues their company may face.

HOW DO YOU MAKE DIGITAL OVERSIGHT WORK IN THE BOARDROOM?

By Betsy Atkins

If there's one thing corporate boards have heard a lot about over the last few years, it's cybersecurity. In my engagements as a director and my work on governance issues, a day doesn't go by without another briefing that tries to tell board members something new about digital and cyber dangers.

We've already heard the hacking horror stories, statistics, and anecdotes, and those are important to understand for managing risk. There is one crucial aspect of board responsibility for digital that does demand more support and guidance from boards: that is establishing the role the board should take in digital oversight and determining what contributions should be expected from the board.

SETTING THE RIGHT TONE FROM THE TOP

It is not the board's role to directly create a company's digital/cyber policy, but rather to ask the right questions and set the tone from the top.

Questions to ask:

- How does our strategy take into account the next digital revolution of IoT, AI, cloud computing, and big data?
- Are we leveraging our data assets to build our business?
- What kind of data do we hold? Where is it housed?
- Who has access, and what is the authentication process?
- Have we segregated our key intellectual property and treated it with higher security?
- What are the firewall/encryption/protocol systems in place, and are these actively monitored?
- How do we review past attacks and responses? Do we establish a cyber-breach response plan? Is it tested?
- Who is directly responsible? Is there a chief information security officer (CISO), and what is the reporting line?

ASKING THE RIGHT QUESTIONS

The ability to ask the right questions requires digital expertise on the board. Since not everyone on the board will be digitally savvy, it's important to touch on this subject at each meeting to build that knowledge. Each board should have at least one digital director, if not two. Good digital oversight can also mean that the board reaches outside for information and validation. The board needs to budget time for outside advisors on digital trends and guidance on looking around the corner at how digital will impact their business models and channels.

Digital expertise is one of the boardroom's newest demand areas, but it's one with vague qualifications. While CFOs are go-to talent for filling a board's need for financial expertise, chief technology officers (CTOs) or CISOs are still uncommon in the boardroom. Despite the "C" in their titles, these execs still aren't at the corporate level of a CFO. They are perceived by some search firms and board members to lack the seniority or seasoning in broader governance oversight to be effective in a board setting, and their tech skills, while solid, may be seen as narrow or limited. A CTO on your board could well be an expert on cybersecurity, data privacy laws, or trending mobile retail opportunities but prove weak on other urgent governance issues.

DETERMINING WHO SHOULD LEAD

How the digital oversight role is filled and led at the board level is also crucial (and often overlooked). Modern corporate boards, especially at public companies, face a huge, demanding workload. A common tactic is to assign digital governance to the audit committee. But audit has increasingly become the board's dumping ground for risky technical matters. Unless you upgrade the committee's skills and capabilities in tech, your digital governance could grow worse instead of better.

Another alternative is to consider chartering a new board committee for tech and innovation. Whichever route you take, be sure to have a committee chair who is savvy in the specific tech issues facing your company and able to lead with a well-planned agenda.

BUILDING RELATIONSHIPS

Finally, remember that your board can't properly oversee digital matters in isolation. First, it needs a solid relationship with your company's tech staff (CTO, CISO, etc.), particularly for the committee chair in charge. Staff's ability to effectively explain technical matters to board members requires tact and emotional intelligence. Skill in building and maintaining these relationships should be reviewed as part of the tech staff's professional organizational development and be part of their evaluation and compensation.

This staff/board interface includes reporting in the slide deck that the board sees on technology matters. Start with careful discussions on the indices the board needs to see, what matters they cover, and how they are reported. Each slide should have a brief, bulleted conclusion at the bottom. Dashboard reporting is useful here, but first devote careful thought to what is to be reported. Be sure you have a summary that explains the insights and recommended actions.

A tech/innovation perspective can be folded into the annual governance committee review on potential board refreshment needs. Your board's evaluation and turnover policies might assure board continuity, but is the board bringing in the fresh skills in tech and other fields the company will need tomorrow? And are you "siloing" board tech oversight but missing its application to other areas, such as shaping future corporate strategy?

Ensuring strong board leadership requires continued education on the impact of a digital strategy on the business, a clear assignment of digital oversight responsibility, and good relations with the IT staff. Well-defined, insightful board reporting on digital info will keep your board informed and ahead of the trends.

This seems like a big shopping list for the board, but once your course is set, it becomes surprisingly simple. If every business today is a digital business, that means every role your board plays must now become part of its digital governance.

Adapted from Digitalist Magazine, November 28, 2018.

KEY TAKE-AWAY

Board-level digital oversight is a new demand that requires tech expertise on the board, understanding the company's digital structure, and setting the tone at the top that digital is an important enterprise risk to be assessed.

FIVE WAYS TO RAISE YOUR BOARD'S DIGITAL IQ

By Betsy Atkins

Technology is disrupting virtually every industry in some way, and a business case for digital literacy on the board is emerging. In this post, I share five ways companies can raise their board's digital IQ.

There can be little doubt in today's business environment that adding board members with broad experience in technology (including software, services, cloud, analytics, and A.I.) will bring critical insights into the boardroom. According to a recent study by Deloitte, the percentage of public companies that have appointed technology-focused board members has grown from 10 percent to 17 percent during the past six years. For high performers—those companies that outperformed the S&P 500 by 10 percent or more for the past three years—this figure almost doubles to 32 percent. However, board refreshment may not happen soon enough for some companies, and adding a few tech experts may not raise the digital IQ of the entire board to a level where decision making becomes nimble. In the interim, the question is, how can companies raise the digital expertise that existing board members bring to the table?

1. CONDUCT A TECHNOLOGY IQ ASSESSMENT

An appraisal of the board's digital IQ should be incorporated into the annual board assessment to identify any areas of weakness. A digital IQ assessment will be different for each board depending upon the company it serves or the industry it operates in, but it may examine some or all of the following elements:

- Are there enough (or any) board members with relevant technology backgrounds?
- Have board members worked within a variety of business models?
- Did board members lead or serve on companies that initiated digital transformation?
- Have board members experienced a significant change in a company's business model?
- How does the board monitor technological innovations and/or looming disruptions?
- Does the board benchmark technology adoption against competitors?
- What metrics is the board tracking to measure progress in digital transformation?
- Does the board meet with the company's CTO or CIO on a regular basis?

2. EMBARK ON A TECHNOLOGY LEARNING CURVE

Every company is a technology company in some way, and all boards should be continuously researching macro trends in technological innovation and digital enablement. An effective way to boost the entire board's digital IQ quickly is a technology learning tour, during which board members spend a few days immersed in one of the major technology hubs, such as Silicon Valley, China, or Tel Aviv.

The board I sit on at Schneider Electric just toured Alibaba in China. We also visited leading Chinese companies in Shanghai, Hangzhou, Shenzhen, and Hong Kong. This fall, I joined my fellow Volvo board members in meetings with Google, Amazon, venture capital groups in Menlo Park, and other cloud services providers as we seek to understand the potential for connected car infotainment. We also met with companies that specialize in machine learning and AI algorithms related to autonomous driving to discern how advances in those technologies may apply to Volvo.

There are major macro tech trends impacting Schneider and Volvo that require their boards to establish a framework of tech knowledge in order to adequately leverage the opportunities these trends present. Schneider for example is an industrial energy management company, and board member knowledge of—and experience with—the industrial internet of things is critical as "hardware" companies like Schneider transition to develop and embed software in their infrastructure.

For Volvo, cloud services, infotainment, SaaS Software, the digital customer journey, and machine learning/algorithms for autonomous drive are all macro trends that are directly relevant to the company's business.

3. INVITE SUBJECT MATTER EXPERTS INTO THE BOARDROOM

Continuing education can take place in the boardroom as well as outside of it. Boards can engage external digital experts to update members about emerging tech-related innovations, disruptions, and risks. Boards should also monitor how competitors are leveraging technology to delight consumers, bring efficiencies to supply chains, and lower costs.

The governance committee of HD Supply brings in outside speakers two or three times a year for a working dinner. We've had cyber-risk speakers from FireEye and digital transformation speakers from Accenture and Boston Consulting Group. An upcoming speaker will be presenting an in-depth discussion of competitive industry assessment.

Internal company technology officers and department heads are also indispensable subject matter experts, and the board should be hearing regularly from the company's top digital managers. (I recently wrote a piece about the evolving role of the CIO.)

The Volvo board's technology and innovation committee regularly receives updates from Volvo's head of research and development, chief digital officer, head of product development, and global head of strategy.

Schneider has created a role of chief digital transformation officer, who reports to the CEO. The Schneider board is considering adding a digital oversight committee.

4. ALLOCATE TIME ON THE BOARD AGENDA TO TECHNOLOGY TRANSFORMATION AS WELL AS CYBER RISKS

There is a lot of buzz right now about cyber risk and how boards should manage oversight of that—and rightly so. However, companies today face a much greater risk than data breaches and ransomware attacks: business model obsolescence. According to a study published by Innosight, businesses are disappearing at a rate of 50 percent every 10 years, primarily because they don't evolve quickly enough in the face of seismic shifts in consumer behaviors or technological innovations (think Blockbuster, Borders, and Radio Shack). Tenure on the S&P 500 has dropped from 33 years to 14 years during the past 7 years.

Companies that seek opportunities for competitive advantage in evolving technologies will have the greatest chance of survival. To ensure business model vibrancy, boards need to embrace tech trends and new business models, and actively consider integration of them into their companies' strategies. Board agendas should allocate time to digital transformation, just as they do cyber, general enterprise risk management, and other risk mitigations.

Digital transformation is a forward-looking perspective, so it shouldn't be tasked to the audit committee (which is traditionally backward-looking). Governance committees, on the other hand, often have additional capacity to absorb tech-related strategic oversight. Governance is the board committee charged with oversight of strategic digital transformation at HD Supply.

As Deloitte reported in the study I referenced at the beginning of this article, it is becoming more common for boards to add technology committees dedicated to digital and technical transformation. Volvo's board has a technology innovation committee, and the Schneider Electric board formed a digital transformation committee.

5. REFRESH THE BOARD WITH DIRECTORS WHO LEAN IN TO CHANGE

The velocity of change is so intense now that corporate survival depends upon the intellectual and emotional experience of people who are more comfortable leveraging change than pulling away from it. To be effective, every director today needs to have past experience navigating a company through rapid and truly transformative change. It's also important that directors in today's business environment have job experience within a variety of enterprises and business models.

If every one around the boardroom table spent their entire career immersed in a single corporate domain or business model, the board may lack familiarity with change or the conviction to innovate. They will try to apply the one lens or framework that was effective one or two decades ago. Board members who have worked for multiple companies during their careers are more likely to have experience leveraging technologies to refresh or retool business models, bring down costs, or improve the customer journey.

Adapted from Nasdaq Global Corporate Solutions, December 19, 2017.

KEY TAKE-AWAY

Raising your board's digital IQ requires first assessing the current skill sets, making digital learning a part of your board's education, and adding new directors who have experienced digital transformation.

THE EVOLVING ROLE OF CIOS AND HOW THE BOARD CAN SPARK TRANSFORMATION

By Betsy Atkins

The past few decades have seen an explosion in the number of C-level roles at the top of global corporations. Many of these are company specific, trendy or just confusing (how is a chief information officer different from a chief knowledge officer?). But the overall trend shows just how complex and specialized running a corporation has become in a time of accelerating, disruptive change. New leaders with new skills truly are needed to survive in this environment—but this also demands regular rethinking of some current C-level roles.

In my role with technology companies (which today means all companies), I've seen this turbocharged evolution hit the role of the chief information officer. Just within the past 12-18 months, the role of the CIO has quickly been transformed.

The CIO office fills a crucial need but may be the wrong "tool" for meeting the demands of the digital business age. The CIO began as a technical pathfinder for companies wrestling with early digital and networking needs. It was viewed as (and typically still is) a back-office, G&A-budgeted function, a cost center supporting SAP/ERP platforms, which today are increasingly legacy systems. The CIO role was measured by the number of company servers, how many employees worked in the data center, and how often someone yelled, "The network is down!"

The past decade has seen the pace of digital change in business push the CIO out of the back office and into a sometimes-uncomfortable new role—the company leader for digital transformation. Once tucked away in the CFO's chain of command, many CIOs now have front-and-center attention and new responsibility for plotting digital strategy.

With new responsibilities for incorporating digital change into strategy, some CIOs are being recast as chief digital officers (CDOs). Traditional responsibilities for overseeing company platforms and systems, while still critical, are gaining powerful added responsibilities under this newly created CDO role.

Sounds impressive, but I've seen many companies struggling, with a CIO role that has one foot still firmly stuck in the past. More of the company's data processing is being outsourced to cloud services like Amazon's AWS, Microsoft's Azure, etc. Also, C-level functions that once depended on the CIO to manage their tech selections are now handling it directly. The chief human resource officer is making the call on new HR platforms (while dealing with issues like online hiring and the gig economy). The chief marketing officer is making the investments in marketing automation and ad tech systems.

Meanwhile, the legacy data systems that are being retained still eat up something like 80 percent of the tech budget, yet they remain crucial to the company's success. Despite their lack of sex appeal, these ERP systems are needed to build products, make payroll, invoice, and all the other basics of any company. Without this basic plumbing (and someone to manage it), none of the fancy sci-fi stuff will happen.

And what about that scary new world with its digital disruptions and opportunities? Technology and digital demands have moved out of the back office to take over the psyche of the C-suite and boardroom. Pioneers like Amazon are shaking up everything we know about retail by erasing the friction, distance, and costs of commerce in sector after sector—and every intelligent business leader today knows his or her sector is next.

Whether your business model is B2C or B2B, rapid, digital upheavals like big data, mobile commerce, cloud computing, AI, and machine learning are now business realities. Whether it's creating a seamless online buying experience, targeting your most profitable customers with artificial intelligence and deep learning insights, or running reverse auction sourcing on the web—it makes no difference. Major companies are realizing that technology is no longer just a back-office cost center—it will either transform you or leave you behind.

To survive in the new business era, a company needs a digital transformation leader. The responsibility of incorporating macro tech trends into company strategy is a role that must be elevated to the highest level of the C-suite. Changing the title and duties of your CIO to chief digital officer may not be enough. A dedicated, planned chief digital role should bring leadership to all of the company's technical and transformative opportunities, serving as a visionary, trendsetter, prod, and "tech consigliere" to the CEO and leadership team.

I see this evolution at work at companies on whose boards I serve. At Schneider Electric, our CIO stepped up to become our effective new chief digital transformation officer. At Volvo, our CIO reports to the new CDO position. My other boards are likewise closely involved in seeking out the digital leadership we know will be needed.

As this suggests, addressing these digital leadership concerns is a board-room matter. What can your board do to oversee digital transformation? As directors, we should lead the strategic discussion on digital transformation, and we should support new company structures, budget, and talent that embrace emerging technology change. Here are some ideas:

Keep abreast of macro tech trends. Support management research on innovative digital business models and ecosystems, such as the marketplace model. For example, should you partner with Amazon and Alibaba or stick with current stocking distributors? Forward-looking boards are creating tech committees to keep track of these trends, incorporate technologies, and measure success. Ask provocative questions. Ask how the company is looking at digital transformation. How does the CIO fit in with coming needs, and what are his/her objectives? Does the current reporting structure enable success? What are we doing to enhance the brand and make our business model more contemporary and effective? How are tech spending budgets reflecting your priorities?

Make sure management is measuring digital success. Metrics like the net promoter score, Klout influencer score, social sentiment score, and conversion of leads can help measure the success of your digital transformation model. Make sure your management team is using such quantitative measurements, analyzing data, and gleaning insights in an effective way. Request that they present this annually at your strategy offsite meeting. Do management rewards, incentives, and promotions push toward innovation—or toward playing it safe?

Ultimately, your company's technology oversight structure reflects how it values that technology. Make sure that this structure is a business enabler, not just a cost center. In today's environment, all organizations need a tech leader who embraces tech trends and actively integrates them into the company's strategy.

Adapted from IT World Canada, October 3, 2017.

KEY TAKE-AWAY

Elevating your IT leader to the C-suite reflects the importance of technology to the company and reinforces its commitment to a strategy that embraces digital transformation.

WHAT DIRECTORS NEED TO KNOW ABOUT DIGITAL ADVERTISING FRAUD

ARE ADS ON FACEBOOK, GOOGLE, AND OTHER PLATFORMS, WORTH IT?

By Betsy Atkins and Sally Hubbard

Earlier this year, Procter & Gamble announced it cut its digital advertising budget by $200 million after putting pressure on social media companies to be more transparent when it came to the reach of the ads they were selling.

"Transparency shined a spotlight on reality and we learned valuable lessons which are driving profound change," said Marc Pritchard, P&G's chief brand officer, according to a Reuters article.

Companies spend huge sums on digital advertising. Proctor & Gamble spent roughly one-third of its $7 billion advertising budget on digital advertising last year.

Most public companies spend hundreds of millions on digital advertising, and it's not often an area of focus for boards.

But a key director role is to perform oversight for the shareholders on how capital is spent. Typically we think of long-term capital allocation for investments, as well as annual operating budget spend, as a key part of the board's oversight.

The large tech platforms have been in the headlines a lot lately, with members of Congress, antitrust experts, and the American public increasingly calling for regulation and antitrust enforcement against them. The rising chorus raises concerns about harms to consumers, competitors, news publishers, and citizens, but has paid less attention to corporate advertisers.

Google and Facebook dominate the $88 billion digital advertising market, accounting for 90 percent of digital advertising growth in 2017 according to Pivotal Research analyst Brian Weiser.[6]

The two tech giants have gobbled up ad dollars, as ad fraud ballooned. Digital ad fraud amounted to $7.4 billion in 2017 and is projected to rise to $10.9 billion by 2021, according to a recent letter sent by U.S. Sen. Mark R. Warner[7] to the Federal Trade Commission. Lacking robust competition in their respective spheres, Facebook and Google face few consequences for rampant ad fraud enabled by their platforms.

Boards of directors are responsible for ensuring that corporate budgets maximize shareholder value, but how can board members ensure that the

---

6 Sarah Sluis, "Digital Ad Market Soars to $88 Billion, Facebook and Google Contribute 90% Of Growth," *AdExchanger*, 10 May 2018, adexchanger.com/online-advertising/digital-ad-market-soars-to-88-billion-facebook-and-google-contribute-90-of-growth/.

7 Mark R. Warner, "Warner Calls on FTC and Google to Address the Prevalence of Digital Ad Fraud," www.warner.senate.gov/public/index.cfm/pressreleases?ID=006515A6-AFFF-4071-B169-D9F6AB170C43.

huge sums spent to advertise through Facebook and Google are getting the returns for shareholders that these platforms self-report?

Google and Facebook have been largely immune to U.S. antitrust enforcement. Modern courts ordinarily require antitrust plaintiffs to prove a price increase or output reduction. Antitrust case law judges anticompetitive conduct and acquisitions through the lens of the "consumer welfare standard" and considers price to be the main measure of consumer welfare. Such a standard has shielded Facebook and Google because the platforms are seemingly "free"—consumers pay with their data, not with money.

Yet Facebook and Google are far from free for advertisers. Rather than solely focusing on the consumer side of the multisided markets of social media and internet search, antitrust enforcers also need to look at competitive harms on the multibillion dollar advertising side.

Digital advertising fraud is rampant. One indicator that corporations are overpaying for advertising through Facebook and Google is the extent of digital ad fraud. The $7.4 billion ad fraud figure quoted in Senator Warner's letter, though not limited to fraud enabled by the tech giants, amounts to an enormous overpayment by advertisers.

Senator Warner's letter came on the heels of a Buzzfeed exposé of a multimillion dollar fraudulent scheme using Android apps.[8] "The revelation of this scheme shows just how deeply fraud is embedded in the digital advertising ecosystem, the vast sums being stolen from brands, and the overall failure of the industry to stop it," according to the article.

Although Warner wrote that there was no evidence that Google had direct knowledge of the scheme, he emphasized that Google's ad network and ad exchanges were implicated. Google controls the vertical stack of the online ecosystem, due largely to its acquisitions of DoubleClick and AdMob. "At

---

8   Craig Silverman, "Apps Installed on Millions of Android Phones Tracked User Behavior to Execute a Multimillion-Dollar Ad Fraud Scheme," *BuzzFeed News*, 18 Nov. 2018, www.buzzfeednews.com/article/craigsilverman/how-a-massive-ad-fraud-scheme-exploited-android-phones-to.

the very least, it seems that across a number of its products Google may have engaged in willful blindness, all while profiting from this fraudulent activity," said the letter.

Facebook, for its part, has admitted to a series[9] of measurement errors in recent years. According to The Register[10], Facebook's audience tool promises advertisers they can reach 41 million 18- to 24-year-olds in the United States, 10 million more than actually live in the country.

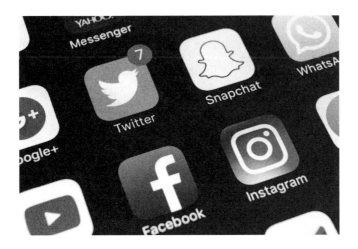

Facebook was sued in 2016 by online marketing agency Crowd Siren for inflating its video view metrics, and after reviewing Facebook's internal documents through discovery, Crowd Siren recently added fraud claims[11] and requested punitive damages. Its amended complaint argues that Facebook knew about the error for a year without telling advertisers, and that Facebook overestimated time spent watching video by as much as 900 percent, not the

9   Tim Peterson, *MarketingLand.com*, 17 May 2017, marketingland.com.

10 Kieren McCarthy, "Facebook Claims a Third More Users in the US than People Who Exist," *The Register® - Biting the Hand That Feeds IT*, 6 Sept. 2017, www.theregister.co.uk/2017/09/06/facebook_claims_more_users_than_exist/.

11 Rachel England, "Facebook Accused of Lying about Video Stats Error for over a Year," *Engadget*, 17 Oct. 2018, www.engadget.com/2018/10/17/facebook-accused-lying-video-stats-year-lawsuit-metrics/.

60 percent to 80 percent figure Facebook had reported. Facebook denies the allegations.

Facebook and Google have suffered few consequences from rampant fraud in part because they lack competitive constraints. Competition presses firms to do better, but Google's and Facebook's ability to track users' behavior across the web creates entry barriers for competition. Both antitrust enforcement and data protection rules that limit Facebook's and Google's ability to track users on others' web properties—like Europe's General Data Protection Regulation—could open up competition.

Transparency and independent verification are necessary. Blind trust in Facebook and Google is both imprudent and inconsistent with the board's enterprise risk management business practices that require independent verification. Boards need to ensure that corporate advertising budgets are getting the right results for shareholders.

In television advertising, advertisers do not merely rely on a network's audience measurement; Nielsen also provides independent measurement, which is then audited by the Media Ratings Council (MRC). But ad dollars continue to move from television to digital, with mobile ad spending expected to surpass television advertising this year.[12]

In 2017, Facebook and Google's YouTube[13] agreed to be audited by the MRC, but the audit is still ongoing. MRC auditing is a step in the right direction, but it does not go far enough. The State of Digital Advertising 2018 report by Marin Software[14], which surveyed over 500 B2C advertising professionals, found that 44 percent of advertisers "feel that the increasing dominance of Google and Facebook will impact their business above all other trends or challenges in 2018."

---

12 "Mobile Ad Spending to Surpass TV in 2018," *EMarketer*, 19 Apr. 2018, www.emarketer.com/content/mobile-advertising-is-expected-to-surpass-tv-ad-spending.

13 https://www.mediapost.com/publications/article/297068/mrc-audits-of-facebook-and-google-whats-at-stake.html

14 "State of Digital Advertising 2018," Marin Software, 2018, www.marinsoftware.com/resources/whitepapers/state-digital-advertising-2018.

As long as advertisers are beholden to Facebook's and Google's self-reported data, their ability to detect fraud and ensure that ad budgets are well spent will be limited.

Board members should demand transparency and third-party verification of advertising data spend. There are often hundreds of millions of dollars spent on digital advertising in order to eliminate fraud and waste from ad budgets. Boards may want to consider asking management to challenge Facebook and Google to use a third-party independent verification company to whom they give real access and transparency into their closed systems.

Adapted from Directors & Boards, December 13, 2018.

KEY TAKE-AWAY

In this digital advertising age, with rampant fraud and domination by Facebook and Google, boards need new, independent verification systems to be sure their companies are getting true value for their digital advertising spend.

THREE WAYS THE TESLA BOARD CAN MITIGATE ELON MUSK'S TWEET DAMAGE

By Betsy Atkins

The SEC is in a quandary as it investigates Elon Musk's ill-advised tweet. Elon Musk's tweet-first/think-later approach may suit his daring personality, but casually tweeting that he had "funding secured" to take a $50 billion public company like Tesla private unleashed a storm of problems for regulators, investors—and his board.

After the U.S. Securities and Exchange Commission began investigating the legality of his announcement, Mr. Musk attempted some damage control in an interview with The New York Times. It essentially amounted to a plea for clemency and mercy from the SEC after an "excruciating" year of work.

We can all applaud Mr. Musk's incredible work ethic, innovative talent, and perseverance. These qualities created a company that has revolutionized the electric car sector (and all while Mr. Musk works to create a private space industry).

Yet it is important to appreciate the quandary these considerations put the SEC in as a regulator. The commission is in the position of potentially shutting down one of the U.S.'s leading innovators over a blatant public disclosure issue that seems to have violated its regulations and that wildly swung the market.

Typical SEC responses would include sanctions or fines against the company in question, the removal of the offending party from serving on a public board, or even seeking to oust the offender from their position.

If, however, the SEC does not punish Mr. Musk, it unleashes a whole new set of dynamics in the public markets. Chief executives might feel free to use social media to move their stock with impunity. The commission cannot apply a regulation selectively; it must be consistent. Giving clemency to the "special circumstances" of a Musk meltdown would mean all public companies should receive the same leniency.

What about the poor, blindsided Tesla board members? They now face a serious damage control effort. A first move that would be well received in the investor community would be to separate Mr. Musk's chief executive role from his Tesla board chairmanship and to designate a new independent chair from within the board.

Many of the current directors are not seen by investors and proxy advisers as being truly independent. The U.S. public pension fund CalSTRS last year insisted two new directors be added: Ebony Media chief executive Linda Johnson Rice, and 21st Century Fox head James Murdoch. And proxy advisers Institutional Shareholder Services and Glass Lewis recommended that investors vote against two out of three directors on Tesla's most recent board slate.

Another mitigation would be to introduce a policy stating that all tweets of a financial nature need to be reviewed and approved, possibly by creating a chief compliance officer role.

This could also be a golden moment to bring in a chief operating officer so that the company can more effectively focus on operations, freeing Mr. Musk up for his best use as a visionary, innovator, and strategist for the brand.

Given the intensity of the public scrutiny the company is under, Tesla's board needs to make fast, bold moves that will help to reassure the SEC. Convincing the regulators (and investors) that the company is in control will be critical for rebuilding confidence and heading off punitive actions.

But such governance decisions would bring long-term benefits too.

Building a reputation for Tesla as not just an entrepreneurial company but also a professional, well-run one will stabilize the business. And the speedy hiring of a respected, well-recognized, manufacturing or automotive industry operator would go a long way to help too. In the immediate future, however, the Tesla board should decide what actions or behavior on Mr. Musk's part might persuade the SEC to be merciful. The coming days and weeks will certainly be a busy time in Tesla town.

Adapted from Financial Times, August 21, 2017.

KEY TAKE-AWAY

The SEC will have to respond to Elon Musk's go-private tweet in an even-handed way to ensure social media doesn't become a tool for CEOs to manage their stock price. The Tesla board will have to do some damage control and come up with a solution on how to reign in Musk's brash antics and they could start by finding an independent chairman of the board.

RETAILERS FACE RADICAL CHANGE . . . AND SO SHOULD THEIR BOARDS OF DIRECTORS, PART 1

By Betsy Atkins

Of the many industries being turned inside out by digital transformation, retailing may face the most radical change. However, it's also the industry with the greatest number of breathtaking new opportunities for success. In this two-part article, I survey the new digital and market forces facing the retail industry, and then detail why fresh leadership (starting at the boardroom level) is needed if you hope to ride this rocket.

The pressures traditional brick-and-mortar retail chains face are obvious and increasing. Many of these have been self-inflicted. The U.S. has far more per capita retail square footage than any other country (six times as much as the UK, for example). In the U.S. alone, 6,700 retail stores are expected to close in 2017.

Meanwhile, the stats for online retail are exploding in ways that both excite and trouble those of us in the sector. U.S. e-commerce sales hit $360.3 billion in 2016 and are expected to reach $462 billion next year. A poll of U.S. shoppers found that 60 percent prefer to avoid crowded malls and stores (which, of course, makes them less crowded), and 71 percent believe they'll find the best deals shopping online. Forty percent of men and 33 percent of women 18 to 34 say that ideally they'd like to buy everything online.

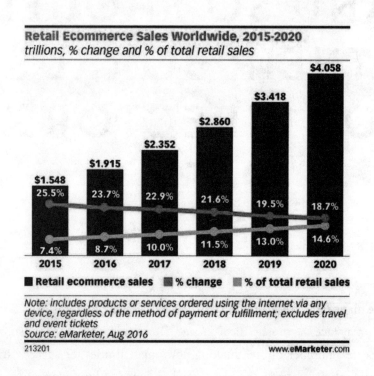

Retail Ecommerce Sales Worldwide, 2015-2020
trillions, % change and % of total retail sales

Note: includes products or services ordered using the internet via any device, regardless of the method of payment or fulfillment; excludes travel and event tickets
Source: eMarketer, Aug 2016

213201   www.eMarketer.com

Those of us who watch the numbers, monitor the trends, and set strategy for retail businesses know they offer an incomplete, even misleading, picture of where the industry in America is headed. First, digital trends are leading us toward a hybrid retailing model built upon both the online and in-store channels but take them in wholly new directions.

First-generation e-commerce was shaped by desktop computing models that are rapidly being outclassed by the rise of mobile commerce. Most growth in online retailing now comes through mobile. Currently, 66 percent of the time U.S. customers spend in retail interaction is on a mobile device. This is higher still in Asia and Europe, pathfinders for this retail innovation. Mobile isn't a supplement to a retailer's online presence; it's now the primary mode, and obsessing over how well your customers can browse, shop, buy, and pay through their smartphones is crucial.

Even that approach is too limited today. Smart competitors (some you may not even realize are competitors) are shaping "omnichannel" digital and hybrid retail models that will surprise and disrupt you tomorrow. Amazon.com and Google invent new ways to source, market, sell, and deliver goods on an almost daily basis. Stitch Fix offers a new apparel retail model using algorithms and artificial intelligence to deliver wardrobe items customized to your profile. Warby Parker brings a similar online shakeup to the staid world of optometry and eyeglasses. Ikea supplements its physical locations with a virtual reality viewer option that lets you remotely browse its stores. Retail spaces will become where shoppers go to learn about products, to be inspired. Retailers will need to sell a story within their store; consumers are demanding experiences as much as purchases.

Pop-up stores, with their temporary, mobile, high-traffic approach, let both mainline and new retailers test products, messages and locations with low cost and high sales per square foot potential. This new $10 billion segment delivers for shoppers seeking seasonal trendy and unique items.

These shoppers are now spoiled. They expect browsing, ordering, payment, and delivery to be painless, fast, and cheap, no matter how they buy. They want and demand omnichannel service. Every time Amazon innovates another "free delivery" model, you face more pressure to meet the online leader head on. Day-to-day purchases will soon offer "self-replenishing" fulfillment. Connected homes, cars, appliances, and products will communicate and transact on their own. Light bulbs, detergent, copy paper, and dog food will order their own replacements, and these meta-service providers will naturally evolve to add other products as well.

The newest hybrid retail innovations bring online and in-store experiences together in fresh ways. More than half of in-store shoppers check prices on their smartphones before buying, and "showrooming" (using local retailers to browse products later bought online) has become the norm.

But online and in-store buying are still tied together. Though 72 percent of younger buyers shop prices online before buying in a physical store, the store is still where they purchase. Over half of shoppers surveyed prefer buying from a source with a physical store presence over an online-only one. Savvy retailers combine bricks and clicks in new ways, such as online purchase options within the physical store, or free delivery of items bought in-store (who wants to lug items around the rest of the day?).

These changes in retail will create a dislocation of retail employees. Some 4.6 million Americans work in retail, making it the country's No. 1 employer. Automated warehouses, drone delivery, robotic customer service staff, and "bot-staffed" call centers will replace the store clerk of old. Companies either must invest in robots right now or prepare to pay more for the best employees.

Adapted from Total Retail, December 13, 2017.

KEY TAKE-AWAY

Mobile has become the first contact method for online retail. The trends in retail are toward a hybrid online/bricks-and-mortar model where the in-store environment must tell a story and create an experience for shoppers to remain engaged.

RETAILERS FACE RADICAL CHANGE . . . AND SO SHOULD THEIR BOARDS OF DIRECTORS, PART 2

By Betsy Atkins

Though the job of a corporate board member has never been easy, show special sympathy for anyone serving as a retailing director over the past few years. The traditional board concerns of retail and measures of success—profit margins, inventory turnover, sales per square foot, traffic, conversions—are under attack by e-commerce. Doing all the traditional things well can leave you in the same position as Kmart, Sears, or The Limited.

These are massive, disruptive, dynamic trends for retailing, but an effective board of directors can help in mastering them. The first question: Who belongs on the ideal retailing board of directors? Most current retail board members made their bones at traditional brick-and-mortar retail companies. They're smart and experienced, but do they have the experience your stores need now? I've found that traditional retail board members are resistant to (and a bit scared of) all the disruptive changes noted in part 1 of this series. For the turbulent world of modern retail, your boardroom talent pool needs to reach beyond the usual suspects to seek candidates who are masters of change.

Add directors with experience in successful, digitally native businesses, with strong knowledge of brand marketing through social media and curating online content that draws buyer loyalty. With customer experience so central to retailing now, adding board knowledge on how consumers interact and make value judgments can prove invaluable. This applies even if the board prospect comes from entertainment, hospitality, technology, or other non-retail fields.

This technology portfolio can offer rich rewards on your board. Artificial intelligence, big data, virtual reality, cybersecurity, drone delivery, marketing automation, the internet of things—all of these technologies are shifting, intersecting, and liberating retail in unforeseen ways, and directors with vitae in these fields can spark your board.

The traditional board role (and talent lineup) focused on a forensic, backward-looking approach, reviewing the past quarter's financials, sales per square foot, and so on. Directors today need to be forward-looking. Where is our consumer and market headed? What new deliverables measure success? What do we need to demolish and rebuild before a competitor does? As an added benefit, recruiting such board talents will shake up board age and diversity concerns.

Such fresh eyes in the boardroom will introduce new languages and concepts of success that retail today must add to its vocabulary. What is your brand's Klout influencer score? Its social sentiment score? How do you measure your company's engagement with its highest-value customers (20 percent of these deliver 80 percent of revenues)? How do you rank in various search engines and retail review sites, and how effectively do you measure online placements and SEO results? It takes boardroom digital IQ just to know which questions to ask.

Next, get your board members (and top managers) out of the office as secret shoppers on the web and in stores. Any retailer that doesn't expect its leadership team to regularly "eat its own dog food" is aiming toward failure. It amazes me how many CEOs never call their own company's call center or try to use their own online ordering system. Assurances that your customers can move seamlessly between PC, tablet, and mobile platforms mean nothing unless you personally try it. If the shopping and order function is clumsy, demands too much time and effort, asks too many questions and then kicks you off at the checkout stage, most top execs and board members will never know.

This is another area where adding board talent with omnichannel retailing skills is so valuable. Your marketing people had better not tell the board how terrific your online presence is if there's a seasoned tech person in the boardroom who's tried it and knows it's clunky. Engaged board members should be supportive of the leadership team in making this new reality happen. They bring an un-conflicted "inside/outside" perspective that's worth its weight in objective gold. When the board speaks, everyone has to listen.

Bringing board talent to your retail evolution is vital today given the stakes involved. Retail bankruptcies are surging, with 20 major chains (including The Limited and Toys "R" Us) on the rocks this year alone. In the early 1990s, business guru Jim Collins wrote that approximately 40 percent of the top companies would be gone in 20 years. Now, I'd say at least half will be gone in 10 years or less.

Your retail company can make the cut, but it may have to completely rethink its locations, brand, market segments, price points, product lines, even its very physical presence. But that's just the sort of top-level, scary strategic discussion a good board of directors should deliver. Directors need to lean in and embrace change, understand, support, and, when appropriate, invest in management proposals to innovate. The biggest part of board oversight is to protect shareholder value. The risk retailers face is staying contemporary and relevant. Directors must help management to future-proof their companies.

Adapted from Total Retail, December 20, 2017.

KEY TAKE-AWAY

All of the macro changes in retail dictate a different digitally savvy board that understands rapid innovation cycles and embraces change. The legacy retail model directors who presided at Sears, Kmart, and Circuit City are not the right "digital" directors to future-proof your company. Board refreshment is tied to success in today's retail reality.

WYNN RESORTS: 7 TACTICS TO CULTIVATE A WORLD-CLASS EMPLOYMENT BRAND

By Betsy Atkins

It's been just eight months since Matt Maddox, CEO of Wynn Resorts (Nasdaq: WYNN), took the reins of the company following the abrupt departure of founder Steve Wynn following sexual misconduct allegations. During that short time, the company's board and leadership team have demonstrated they are serious about creating a workplace that fosters diversity and inclusion.

Perhaps the most public example of that commitment is the swift nomination and on-boarding of three new women board members: Betsy Atkins, Dee Dee Myers, and Wendy Webb. NASDAQ reached out to the newly minted Wynn board members, to learn more about the multi-faceted approach the company is taking to restore its employment brand and the trust of all its stakeholders, from shareholders to front-line employees.

They shared seven tactics that Wynn has employed to emerge from the crisis stronger than ever—and with a world-class employment brand that maximizes its diverse talent pool.

1. SEPARATE THE CEO AND CHAIRMAN ROLES.

When Steve Wynn stepped down, naturally there was concern that Wynn Resorts would have a difficult time separating the man from the brand—the very logo of the company is his signature. However, Matt Maddox, Wynn's new CEO, has spearheaded a smooth succession—in part because the board separated the roles of chairman and CEO when Steve Wynn stepped down.

The on-boarding of a new CEO is a key opportunity for companies with a combined chairman/CEO role to consider separating that role. Wynn's board elected to split the roles, as they wanted to allow Matt to focus on leading the company through a potentially bumpy transition period. "Matt has taken this transition very seriously, devoting a lot of time in person engaging with employees to listen to them and to share his vision for the company going forward," shared Betsy Atkins. "And when you look at the company's recent performance, Wynn hasn't missed a beat: The overall performance of the company has remained strong and the corporation continues to function smoothly."

2. BRING MEANINGFUL GENDER DIVERSITY TO THE BOARD.

The Wynn Resorts leadership team committed to bringing a new perspective to company leadership and the board as the company turned its focus internally on gender diversity, inclusion, and sensitivity. The board recruited Betsy Atkins, Dee Dee Myers, and Wendy Webb through a very robust and transparent process, during which the entire board was fully engaged. Adding three new independent women directors placed the company among the top 40 of S&P 500 companies (by female board representation).

Women in S&P 500 Companies

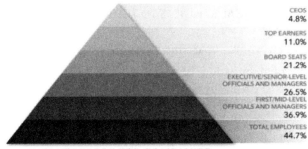

CEOS
4.8%

TOP EARNERS
11.0%

BOARD SEATS
21.2%

EXECUTIVE/SENIOR-LEVEL
OFFICIALS AND MANAGERS
26.5%

FIRST/MID-LEVEL
OFFICIALS AND MANAGERS
36.9%

TOTAL EMPLOYEES
44.7%

WOMEN IN S&P 500 COMPANIES

Sources

Catalyst, *Women CEOs of the S&P 500* (2019).
EY Center for Board Matters, 2016 Top Earners in S&P 500 Companies, Unpublished data.
Catalyst, *2016 Catalyst Census: Women and Men Board Directors* (2017).
U.S. Equal Employment Opportunity Commission (EEOC), Unpublished 2015 S&P 500 EEO-1 data.

S&P 500 is owned by S&P Dow Jones Indices, LLC.
Updated: 16 January 2019

CATALYST.ORG

"There are mountains of evidence that show conclusively that diverse groups of decision-makers make better decisions. So diversifying the Wynn board quickly in the wake of Steve Wynn's departure was essential to navigating the crisis," said Dee Dee Myers. "Betsy, Wendy and I not only bring our unique perspectives and experiences to our roles, but we also bring new skills, and that has been helpful as the board develops and rolls out strategies to address a range of challenges, from improving workplace diversity and inclusion, to compliance, compensation, and communications."

"Adding three new directors at once—let alone three new women directors—changes the dynamics in any boardroom," said Betsy Atkins. "However, we were warmly received, and the board's timing has allowed Dee Dee, Wendy, and me to be part of the launch of a whole new set of diversity and inclusion initiatives, both from an oversight as well as a participation standpoint. Wynn's board and leadership team are moving quickly to ensure the company and its employees come through this transition stronger than ever, and I'm thrilled to be a part of that work."

3. RECRUIT CRITICAL SKILLSETS TO THE BOARD.

With its new women board members, Wynn not only improved the board's gender profile, but added skillsets that will be instrumental in guiding the company going forward. Dee Dee Myers and Wendy Webb each have high PR profiles that can help to bolster Wynn's brand halo. They also bring critical crisis management, strategic communications, and PR skillsets that the board can leverage to help Wynn communicate its new strategies and navigate the leadership transition smoothly.

Wynn Resorts is actually five businesses in one: entertainment, retail, hospitality, gaming, and dining, so there are myriad ways the company can leverage the talents and expertise of its new board members. Wendy spent 20 years as a senior executive at The Walt Disney Company, so she has an entertainment and direct-to-consumer perspective that is valuable on the Wynn Resorts board.

"I'm excited to bring to the Wynn Resorts board not only my experience in global travel & tourism learned over two decades at Disney, but also knowledge about the nuances associated with transitioning from a founder-led company to the next phase of professional management," said Wendy Webb. "Additionally, given my background in Investor Relations and Strategy, and through service on other public company boards, I recognize the importance of maintaining a sharp focus on creating value for shareholders. It is through this lens that I have approached my duties as a Wynn board member, while not losing sight of this company's culture and core values that make it a leading brand in the hospitality industry."

Dee Dee also brings considerable experience in public relations, messaging, transition management, and crisis management. She is currently executive vice president for worldwide corporate communications and public affairs at Warner Bros. Entertainment, so she is very familiar with the ripple effects of #MeToo issues.

Betsy Atkins's background as a veteran board member and a tech entrepreneur with experience with digital transformation, AI, branding, retail e-commerce, and creating seamless omnichannel consumer experiences can be applied a number of ways to Wynn's business lines.

4. BENCHMARK THE CURRENT CULTURE.

The board and management team of Wynn are committed to having a workplace where every employee feels safe, supported, and has equal opportunities to develop his or her full potential. The first thing Matt and his leadership team did was benchmark the current culture.

Wynn conducted an employee-wide survey based on Fortune's "100 Best Companies to Work For" survey, adding questions related to diversity, working women, harassment, discrimination, and women's leadership opportunities to get a full baseline of how employees perceive the culture and working environment at Wynn Resorts. The leadership team has done a preliminary read-out of the results. Several focus groups have been created, each working on the departments that have the biggest impact on the employee base.

In addition, Wynn has engaged a compensation consultant to conduct a comprehensive pay equity study and a promotion equity study to review the rate of succession by gender and by ethnic groups. The company is also working with the Secretary of State of Nevada to participate in their gender equity workplace study.

"When I was approached about joining the board of Wynn Resorts, I quietly paid a visit to the Wynn Las Vegas property," said Betsy Atkins. "I wanted to get a read on its front-line employee base. Wynn is a premium hospitality company, delivering boutique luxury hotel service on a massive 4,000+ room scale—which means service employees are the core asset of the company's brand halo. At every level and every touch point at Wynn Las

Vegas, I was consistently met with employees who were clearly happy to be working at Wynn and who truly cared about their customers. Whatever issues Wynn would face in the fallout of its founder stepping down, a demoralized and indifferent employee base wasn't one of them—a fact that reinforced my decision to join the company's board of directors."

5. CREATE A NEW DIVISION FOCUSED ON LEADERSHIP DEVELOPMENT.

Wynn has created a new division, the Culture and Community Department, which is specifically focused on leadership and development, diversity and inclusion, community relations, and gender equality. The entire 25,000 employee workforce of Wynn will feel the impact of the rollout of this division.

As part of this initiative, Wynn launched a Women's Leadership Council, and all four women directors (there was already one woman on the board, Patricia Mulroy) participated in the kickoff and will be involved going forward. The council will host town hall meetings, chats, and networking events to promote advancement of the female employee base.

Wynn is also expanding its already robust internal organizational development program to include leadership development curriculum that covers its broad employee base. There are classes that develop interns into first-time leaders, courses to develop supervisors and managers, courses for rising directors and senior VPs, and training for junior executives reporting to Wynn's C-suite.

6. ROLL OUT A COMPREHENSIVE COMPLIANCE AND EDUCATION PROGRAM.

Wynn Resorts has revisited and updated its internal employee code of conduct and associated training and taken that process a step further by adding specific diversity and inclusion courses. The content and complexity of the courses are tailored by the level of employee: directors and above take an eight-hour course; first-line managers or supervisors take a four-hour course; and line-level employees in hospitality, restaurants, or retail take a two-hour course.

The curriculum includes subconscious bias awareness, updated anti-sexual harassment and compliance training, and very comprehensive reporting training for management. An outside firm is implementing the program, which is supervised and owned at the senior level of Wynn's internal human resource and legal departments.

7. REBUILD TRUST WITH SHAREHOLDERS AND FOSTER SUPPORT FOR LONG-TERM STRATEGIES.

As Wynn's leadership team began rolling out internal strategies to bolster trust with employees and consumers, the board participated directly in the most recent proxy outreach season. The goal was to update shareholders on how the company's leadership team is navigating the leadership transition and to generate support for the new long-term strategies the company is implementing to ensure the employee brand is strong.

Board members had face-to-face conversations with several big index funds, including Vanguard, State Street Global Advisors, and BlackRock. Along with Wynn's general counsel and CFO, board members also had conversations by phone with institutional shareholder corporate governance and proxy voting groups.

* * *

Betsy Atkins serves as President and Chief Executive Officer at Baja Corp, a venture capital firm. She is currently on the board of directors of Wynn Resorts, Schneider Electric, Cognizant, and a private company, Volvo Car Corporation, and served on the board of directors of The Nasdaq Stock Market LLC and as CEO and board chairman at Clear Standards.

Margaret J. "Dee Dee" Myers has been Executive Vice President, World-wide Corporate Communications and Public Affairs for Warner Bros. Entertainment, a broad-based entertainment company and division of TimeWarner, Inc., since September 2014. She also serves on the board of the National Museum of American History. Myers served as White House Press Secretary under President Bill Clinton during his first term.

Winifred "Wendy" Webb has been Chief Executive Officer of Kestrel Corporate Advisors, an advisory services firm counseling corporate and non-profit organizations on strategic business issues, including growth initiatives, digital marketing, board governance, and investor relations, since February 2013. Ms. Webb currently serves on the boards of ABM Industries (since 2014) and 9 Spokes (since 2015). She also serves as co-chair of Women Corporate Directors, Los Angeles/Orange County Chapter.

Adapted from Nasdaq Clearinghouse, October 4, 2017.

KEY TAKE-AWAY

Wynn Resorts Inc. is an example of a company that has embraced the opportunity to enhance and improve its company culture with the departure of its founder and CEO. The company has made significant commitments to diversity at all levels starting with the addition of three new female board members.

MACHIAVELLI
IN THE
BOARDROOM

*It may not be stilettos and poison rings, but new
CEO/princes face real boardroom dangers.*

By Betsy Atkins

In my career as a company founder, venture capitalist, and corporate director, I've met many business leaders, thinkers, and doers. All have offered
good advice on launching, managing, and monitoring an enterprise. But
many of these leaders are a bit shy on sharing insights on a tricky, but important, aspect of leadership—how the savvy chief executive manages his or
her board of directors. So, I thought I'd check in with one particular longtime

acquaintance on high-stakes career management in the real world. Niccolò Machiavelli, 15th-century Italian diplomat, courtier, and author of *The Prince*, thoughtfully answered my email (on parchment, no less) on how our modern boardroom princes should use realpolitik to survive and thrive:

"Thank you for your query, Betsy, and for the information you thoughtfully included. If the longevity of CEO positions today has truly declined to 4.5 years, it would seem that the overthrow of sovereigns now is even more common than in the time of the Medicis (albeit less deadly).

"There seem to be various factors in making the modern chief executive short-lived. The most frequent cause of CEO turnover is company underperformance relative to peers (though there seem to be many exceptions to this rule). The board of directors then may lose confidence in the prince, particularly if shareholders are raising a din outside the castle gates.

"However, the board of directors of the enterprise may bring less-democratic impulses to their governance role. CEOs of companies that feature a separate board chair, particularly a founder or emeritus chairman, are especially vulnerable. This powerful, independent boardroom leader's views carry great weight with the other directors, and he can be mercurial in his support or opposition to the chief. Though a founder may have been the incoming CEO's sponsor or mentor, he can prove fickle if the founding legacy seems at risk and may do a turnabout to lead a boardroom rebellion.

"While the founder or emeritus chair may claim the highest of motives for such a revolt, we often find the replacement CEO to be none other than the founder or emeritus chair himself. Indeed, it is quite possible that any of the princelings gathered around that board table may in fact be seeking the crown. The ideal director is a current or recent CEO with fresh experience, mentoring ability, and the perspective of a business leader who's 'been there, done that,' in the current phrase. This makes them estimable board members—and, likewise, ideal interim CEOs. Recent figures show that about one-fifth of U.S. CEO turnover finds the job taken by a current board member. Novice CEOs, in particular, may face directors who are not thinking, *How can I help this CEO do a better job?* but rather, *I should be the one doing this job!*

"Thus, the new CEO/prince faces real boardroom dangers. However, there are a few tactics he or she should exercise that will help. First is to announce the desire to refresh and renew the board to make it a stronger partner in governance. Second is to encourage board evaluation and director succession planning—which, of course, will lead to some board turnover. Even two or three new board members can help reshape the board's perspective and better align it with the new CEO's vision. Of course, it will not harm the new CEO's cause if these new members not only share his or her strategic goals but are also allies.

"Board renewal and best practices should shift membership in other ways. Even if a founder or emeritus chair is the new CEO's current supporter, governance best practice seeks to retire such veterans from the board. Done right, the board will seek the good governance benefits of the founder's retirement—and relieve the new CEO of a potential threat.

"I should note, however, that the modern board of directors, particularly those of public companies, no longer accepts their past status as lapdogs for a powerful chief executive. Poor performance will lead any board today toward rebelliousness. My era offered the handy leadership tools of the Borgias to enforce discipline: stilettos and poison rings. CEOs now must survive through less exciting measures, such as solid EPS and share price. However, that should not mean ignoring political boardroom realities that can help improve their odds."

Adapted from Directors & Boards, April 2014.

KEY TAKE-AWAY

Board refreshment is a key factor in determining CEO tenure. Within 18 months of becoming CEO, you should have replaced at least one-third of your board.